MUM'S THE
Word!

Pat,
I pray
you are inspired
by my s

Lorna Little

Love wins!.

MUM'S THE
Word!

A memoir of family secrets reveals the complexities of love, relationships, and coming to terms with change.

Lorna Little

- A Memoir -

All photographs courtesy of the author.

MUM'S THE WORD!
Copyright © 2014 by Lorna Little

Mailing address: A Little Guidance, LLC.
P.O. Box 270092
West Hartford, CT 06127-0092

First Edition
Cover Illustration Copyright © 2014 by Alonzo Little
Book Design and Production-AL Conceptz...
Editing by Adam Zinkievich

ISBN-13: 9780986174452
ISBN-10: 0986174459

-ACKNOWLEDGEMENTS-

This book is lovingly dedicated to my mom, Alice Brown.

I would like to express my gratitude to the people who helped me through the completion of my book, to all those who kept mum, yet provided support, read drafts, offered comments, gave written remarks, and assisted in the editing, and design. Adam Zinkievich, my editor, has traveled this journey with me over the past few years; Yvonne Renee Davis provided support, guidance, and written feedback throughout the process; more recently, Rev. Shelley Best gave me her feedback with candor and love; Dr. Alice Farrell and Alicia Little Hodge provided clinical information for the accompanying workbook; Jeannette Horton, the book club queen, offered her insights; and Dr. Stanley Battle, Rev. Ronald Holmes, June Archer, and Bishop James B. Walker, respectively presented the academic, spiritual, and male perspectives. I am additionally thankful to close friends who also recently learned of my story through conversation or by reading a draft copy of this book. Your loving, supportive non-judgmental responses provided encouragement as I released my story to the world.

A special thank you to the New York Times Best-selling author, Victoria Rowell, as her words so eloquently provided a beautiful review for the book. Darryl (D.M.C.) McDaniels, a founding member of the pioneer Hip Hop group RUN-D.M.C., provides the foreword for the book -from a perspective that echoes and connects with everyone, especially adoptees worldwide. Thank you for sharing your words; your truth. I am blessed to have your support. Another special thank you goes to Karen Caffrey, who gave my book another review, and our reconnecting is another example of an "ordaincident" (you'll see these little God moments throughout my book), as I hadn't seen or spoken to her since our telephone conversation over 16 years ago, and just as I brought this book to a close, she so happens to be a speaker at a meeting I attended.

I would like to thank my biggest supporter, my dear husband, Alonzo, for sharing and helping to make it an amazing life. With him by my side, I have lived the words in this book, and his support has enabled me to get this book published. He is my partner in every sense and will always do everything possible to assist me in making my dreams a reality. I thank my girls for allowing me to share my story, and in turn put their lives in the spotlight. Additionally, I thank my family members for understanding my need to write this book; thank you for allowing me to fulfill my purpose.

Above all, I would like to thank God for giving me the courage and the strength to jump off of the cliff and spread my wings; embracing my flight, the soar, and the freedom.

Lastly, if I have not mentioned you by name, please blame my mind and not my heart.

Thank you, the reader, for expressing interest in my book and for co-signing the unmasking of secrets and lies to embrace our truths.

-FOREWORD-

This book is a must read for ALL people. This story is a story that relates to us all.

The truth of who we are is very complex and many times our lives turn into the movie of the week.

Just ask yourself "Who am I?" And start to investigate yourself.

Check your resume and then go back and fact check, I guarantee you will discover things that you never knew even existed.

This is one individual journey that represents the journey of us all.

As you read this book just ask yourself "What would I do if all this happened to me?"

Lorna's story is interesting and inspiring and I believe that it will encourage all those who dare to come on this journey with her to find out things about themselves.

All of our lives are full of secrets and mysteries and all of those

secrets and mysteries are our truth!

"MUM'S THE WORD" are the words for all of us!!!

Are you ready?

Darryl McDaniels
a.k.a. DMC, of pioneering
Hip-Hop group RUN-DMC

-PROLOGUE-

In the end, writing something so challenging came easier to me than I had thought, even though it required me to present my secret thoughts, feelings, and emotions on the world's stage. While I originally wrote down my story to provide me with a personal release, I realized it needed to be shared further for me to truly feel free. This story is deeply rooted and will not only help others, but will also completely free me from feeling burdened by longstanding secrecy. This memoir will allow me to share with you what I have only been able to share with few.

"Mum's the Word" is the title that God led me to share my story through, as silence is what has been required of my secret, until now. "Mum's the Word" is also a part of the spoken debt I owed to my mother. It should come as no surprise that mum is also a term often used in Europe, meaning mother. Therefore, the title truly brings my life, my story, full circle. How ironic a word known for keeping quiet is also a homonym for mother, a word I used to keep me silent, a word also a part of my beginnings, my birth, and my life. It is a word that has now come into full bloom, just like a beautiful chrysanthemum.

This book will provide you with hope as you journey through my trials and tribulations, experiencing surprises, while uncovering secrets, as I return to them as they often return to me. After this experience, you too will exhale cathartically; having the knowledge that humankind can make it through anything. Humanity will persevere.

As human beings, I believe our paths are predestined, and we have to energize our purpose at every stage of our lives. What we do for fun, work, and worship, it all ties back to who we are, who we were born to be, and who we will become. I invite you to open your mind and discover more about yourself as you read of my own self-discovery.

Discovery will come even easier for those who have shared an unexpected life event, a circumstance often filled with questions. Why was I placed here? It is these situations that add another dimension to the question posed by Dr. Rick Warren within the very title of his book, "The Purpose Driven Life: What on Earth am I Here For?"

Confronting these questions allows us to learn more about ourselves, as we share collectively the universal human experience. It is up to us how we choose to enjoy the passage toward resolutions and who we bring with us along the way. I am glad to be sharing my journey with you.

-CHAPTER 1-
WEDDING PRESENT

Before the completion of this book, silence was largely golden, but the impact of the secret that had been revealed to me in 1997 was about to be felt by another member of my family. As a family, we were a private people, but this was no moment to keep quiet. It was a time of joy, where my eldest daughter, Alicia, was marrying the love of her life. He was a military man who was going to be stationed overseas. As a result, what I was about to share could not wait. My secret had to be revealed before she left the country.

To complement the occasion, I wanted her to know, I felt obligated to tell her, how she had a support system that she was wholly unaware of, some individuals I myself had for a long time been oblivious to. Her wedding was truly beautiful: fresh flowers, the pretty coral bridesmaid dresses, and the reception that everyone enjoyed so much.

This support system included Sharon and her beautiful daughter, Karen, who had also attended Alicia's wedding, just not introduced as who they really were. Rather, Sharon was introduced as her cousin from England. The situation had brought me back to recalling a time when another member of that support system, Linda, had come to visit, and I so desperately wanted to tell my children the truth then as well. However, I kept reminding myself that I had been asked to maintain secrecy. It was now that the significance of this otherwise rarely-disclosed information would help her if she ever needed it, if she was to ever become homesick.

Several days after I released my oldest daughter through marriage, I felt it was time to free the secret I could no longer contain from her. Although part of me hesitated over how there would be plenty of other times to share it later, she was married now, and, ironically, moving to the same part of the world where most of my secret resided, the United Kingdom. My daughter was moving to an area where she would otherwise have no idea a support system even existed.

With my thoughts distressed in restlessness, I was sitting on the edge of a seat in my home. My fidgeting hands were folded impatiently in my lap in the family room, as I stared anxiously at the clock. My mind was jumping like an unbridled horse, and my heart was beating so hard I could hear it thumping in my chest. Although the repercussions of what I was about to do were uncertain, there was no turning back. I needed to move forward and pray for the best.

Worried by the possible outcomes of my revelation to come, I was waiting for my husband, Alonzo, to arrive home and reassure me one more time how I was making the right decision. We had both decided that on this day we would tell our daughter about this well-kept secret together. When she shared with us that she would be moving to England after her wedding, my husband and I had talked about how important it would be to share it with her. Once he came home, he looked at me and asked if I was sure this was what I wanted.

Hesitantly, I responded, "Yes?"

He was nervously tapping his foot to a beat of anxiety as we waited for her to show up. Then, I heard the doorbell ring! Without hesitation, I ran upstairs, only to realize the ringing sound was just coming from the television. Although I had mustered up the courage, in that split second, when no one was there, my previous unresolved emotions considered resurfacing. However, I did not want to lose the focused adrenaline and certainty I just had.

Luckily, I would not have to. As I turned to go back downstairs, a doorbell rang again. This time, it was our doorbell. She was here. With a deep breath, I gradually opened the door.

She greeted me, "Hey ma."

I replied, "Hey, come in and let's go downstairs."

Her husband, Lamont, was not with her. We felt she could tell him herself when she chose to at her leisure. We descended into our basement. It was almost time to tell her the truth. Although my unease began returning as we walked downstairs, seeing Alonzo reminded me of why we were there, how this event, this moment, was meant to be. We sat down. The stage had been set. Lights, camera, action!

Alonzo and our daughter exchanged hellos. I could not delay any longer, starting by telling her there was something we would like to share with her. The matter was led up to by telling her how proud we were of her and her accomplishments: graduating from college with honors, getting married to a respectable man, and taking a major leap in independence by moving thousands of miles away. Beyond the silence that followed, there was now no turning back. I glanced at my husband for support. He looked at me lovingly and nodded me on.

I continued, "Since you will be moving to England, there is something that I want to tell you," to which she said, "What is it?"

I could tell that she had now detected our discomfort.

I sat up straight and started with "…you know, first of all, what I am going to tell you I have only known since May of 1997. I also want you to know that I too am still processing this information, which I only found out accidentally." I felt this would prevent one of my biggest fears from becoming a reality, her feeling as if everyone had been lying to her since her birth. I did not want her to experience what that felt like, what I felt when I found out the truth.

"Do you remember when I told you about your cousins Sharon and Linda? I had told you how we were related, but what I told you was not the entire truth." I felt a mixture of stress and relief when the secret then poured forth from my mouth. The secret was making a rare public appearance.

She had a puzzled look of bewilderment on her face, trying to grasp what was now the truth, as she replied, "How did that happen?"

It was clear that she was internally spinning over the same thoughts I felt when I first found out, trying to make sense of what seemed absurd. I nervously began to answer her and explain the whole situation in detail. During this time, my daughter did not appear visibly upset, just bewildered by this new information presented.

She said, "I noticed a strong resemblance and felt a strange connection with my two cousins." " Is July still my cousin?"

I told her, "Your grandmother is not keen on talking about the details."

It was also my father not being alive that really made the whole truth likely hidden forever. Had he still been alive when I had found out, he was someone so easy to talk to I could imagine him then sharing everything. I reminded her that I knew this was a lot to take in, but I felt she should know that she had individuals who she could turn to while she was living overseas. I also said it would be a good time to get to know them, and hopefully, they would be able to grow an honest relationship while she was there.

I explained to her who I believed also knew this secret and who did not and invited her to ask any questions she might have. We went on to have a beneficial exchange of questions and answers, with me never doubting my decision once it had been made. Through this disclosure, we wanted to make sure she did not feel distant from anyone in our family afterward. Although having finally shared this secret with Alicia was a relief, which she now also had to carry, to truly know how I was feeling that day and to experience the magnitude and repercussions of the secret as I did, I need to start from the beginning.

-CHAPTER 2-
CLOUD FORMATION

I began to accidentally stumble on this secret in March of 1997. My family on my mother's side was having a reunion outside of the United States. Some of our family had decided to come together in Jamaica for a tropical reunion. I decided I wanted our family to attend, which had caused me to need a new passport.

Prior to this time, I had not traveled overseas in over 15 years. Excited, I knew it would be a memorable experience. This was the first time my mother's side was hosting such large gathering. I was worried most about not getting a passport in time.

Although my family was from Jamaica, I had only gone there once before, when I was younger. I had heard all of the family stories about how my mother had 12 brothers and sisters and how close they all were growing up. Most of my cousins that I knew were the offspring of my mother's many siblings. It was this rich heritage that I wanted to share with my two children and husband who had never been to Jamaica before.

I had been born in England and lived there for six years, until immigrating to the United States, where I lived for most of my life. Most of the people I knew who came here from other countries were considered resident aliens. This meant that although they could legally live here, they were not citizens of the United States, which is why I had to get my British passport. As it turned out, mine had expired many years ago. Making the application process easier, since I was an adult, I did not need to ask my mother for any documents to reapply.

In order to complete my passport application, I first needed to obtain my birth certificate. Upon collecting the necessary information, it was time to send my request off to the British Consulate. I was born in England and was a Green Card holder in the United States. As there would not be enough time to obtain American citizenship first, I had to send my information to the U.K.. I prayed I would still have enough time.

As I prepared to send out my request, thoughts of family bonding and connectedness flowed through my mind. Something inside of me caused me to feel that this family reunion would be even more special than all of those that had come before it. Most of my familial contact had been with my mother's family. Except for my uncle in Pennsylvania, aunt in Germany, and a few cousins in Connecticut, I was not as close to my father's side. This was primarily because they were living all over the globe.

The information package was sent off in a white envelope with a few air-mail stamps, with no major expectations or anticipated issues after that. This was just a routine step needed for completing my passport application that would allow me to attend a family reunion.

As the days went by, the wait made it hard to concentrate at work and at home. At the time, I was working in the human services field as a Program Manager. In this role, I assisted clients with a variety of mental health issues, including work-related stress, substance abuse, and family problems. In general, I helped people obtain and maintain a sense of normalcy and peace, aiding them in achieving a more normal-steady state. I enjoyed helping people answer questions in their lives.

Overall, my professional work had always been extremely important to me – as if it had been a calling for me to help people overcome their struggles. My work had served as ministry toward helping people "get back to normal," or as close to it as possible. The crises and challenges, ups and downs, and disappointments and disruptions that clients experienced on a daily basis were presented to me for guidance, assistance, and referral. I was happy to assist and always felt blessed to be able to have a manageable, emotionally non-eventful life.

Anxiously waiting for the family reunion, I could not pursue booking airline tickets until I received my birth certificate – which the wait for it began to feel like forever. I even called to see what was taking so long – as deadlines continued to draw nearer as my nervousness mounted. When I spoke to the woman at the consulate and inquired about the status of my birth certificate, she said it had taken longer than anticipated to research, but that it was now in the mail. Feeling reassured how at least the process was continuing in motion, I expressed my gratitude to her that it was on the way. I then proceeded to eagerly wait for its arrival.

Like a child waiting for Christmas Day to come, five days later the package finally arrived in a large brown envelope, adorned with the colorful and ornate Royal coat of arms of the United Kingdom. On the day of the certificate's arrival, my husband and I had planned to go to my oldest daughter's open house at her school. She had a science experiment that was going to be exhibited as part of the evening's activities. Our plan was to come home and quickly grab dinner and snacks for our two kids, then hastily head out to catch the scientific demonstrations.

Smiling at the beautifully-sealed envelope, I marveled at how the British do everything with such class. I even thought to myself that I would become a dual citizen of both countries; to me it just felt like being a member of royalty if you were a citizen the United Kingdom. However, fleeting and fanciful thoughts that carried me away were suddenly erased when I opened the parcel and saw what was inside. It was information that quickly grounded me, although it felt hardly like reality and much more like a bad dream.

Staring down at my certificate, I whispered confused to myself, "Certificate of Adoption?"

Then, gasping, in a louder decibel, I remarked that these people from the U.K. are so disorganized, sending me the incorrect documentation, etc.

I thought to myself, "What am I going to do now? I cannot meet all of the other deadlines needed to make this family reunion with this terrible mistake."

This was a sad and sorry excuse for not finding my proper birth papers. For them to take so long, only to give me incorrect documentation was maddening. I was now back to square one, with less than five days before I had to confirm my attendance at my mother's family reunion.

Giving the U.K. one more chance, I looked at the certificate again more closely. It did have both my mom and dad's names on it, which made sense, but they were listed as my adoptive parents. It had my birth date and name. I became dizzy and angry at what I thought was still a very odd mistake or someone playing a practical joke. I sent out for one simple request and ended up with what I thought was an invalid document. Or was it? I paced back and forth more uneasily the longer I looked at it. My body was pulsing with unanswered emotions.

Shortly thereafter, my pacing ceased. I now could not move. I had become a statue upon realizing the life-changing magnitude of what this sudden shock of information meant. Dazed, I experienced full-fledged cognitive dissonance, at the thought of having two mothers, as I began to feel just like my clients who contacted our agency when in crisis. "How would I console someone in my situation? This is a big, big mistake. This can't be – adoptive parents?" I repeated this last phrase over and over again in my head.

My heart beat louder and louder, having now moved inside my throat, obstructing my ability to breathe. I soon heard it pounding in my ears, wanting to escape. My daughter's school presentation was in the far recesses of mind. We were running late, but I could not move. It was as if the past that I knew had become one big play. What was real and what was only acting?

I could not tell you what my daughter's display would be about. Although I knew, my mind and my reality were temporarily unpredictable. Somehow I regained the ability to move and make my way out of the house. We were soon in the car, but I could not speak, not even to my husband.

"Baby, is there something wrong. You aren't yourself. Are you okay?" He asked me twice more before I could even begin to summon the strength to respond.

Before we could go to the school, we had to stop and pick up my mother. My stomach was tight the entire ride. Although I felt nauseous, I could not throw up. What was happening to me? How could this be? I share everything with my husband, and under normal circumstances, I would have blurted discoveries of this magnitude out without questioning or looking back, but our children were present. This new information was too much to just blurt out. I mumbled to him that it was something stupid due to incompetent people and would tell him about it later.

When we finally picked up mom, still in confusion and disbelief, I could not bear to look at her. She noticed I was looking strangely past her instead, but I felt this was the easiest way to avoid asking questions in front of everyone. Now in motion, the drive seemed like it had become a never-ending road trip, and the once familiar Route 44 in Avon, Connecticut, was now a disorienting and foreign blur of trees and rock formations. My mind continued to race faster than the car was driving us. I began to question so many things that I had thought to be true and secure for so long, for as long as I could remember. Things I had always believed in.

Although I kept quiet, I was screaming inside my head, trying to rationalize what I had just found out, "This can't be!"

I said a few statements in the car in a "no big deal" tone

to see if it elicited any response from my mom. In one instance, I mentioned, "I sent off for my birth certificate so I can get my passport for our family reunion. I don't know why it is taking so long."

All she said back was, "Oh yeah?" in the most nonchalant manner imaginable at the time. Such a flat response seemed to satisfy the part of me in internal denial that this was all just a big misunderstanding, unless my mother was an expert at keeping secrets. The information must have just been entered incorrectly. Everything would continue on as usual once things were fixed. Could things be fixed?

We finally arrived at the school. At least the car ride was over, which had included my husband again seeing right through my front and saying, "What's the matter? You don't seem like yourself."

Still trying to figure things out to myself, I kept replying, "Everything is fine; I'm just tired." However, I was covering up and he knew it.

I went through our initial entrance into the school distracted and wondering if this could be true. Could I actually be adopted? Is this woman sitting next to me not my mother? Was my late father really my father? I mean, I looked like him for crying out loud! It must be a mistake.

For the next two and half hours, I was living in suspended animation; floating above the crowd of parents observing and asking simpler questions about their children's science fair presentations. No one else was currently questioning who their parents were. I could not even grasp what my daughter was doing. At one point that night, seeking comfort from mental turmoil, I reached out and gave my eldest daughter, Alicia, a huge hug and kiss to feel an embrace that was undeniably between a mother and her daughter.

During my moments of clarity through this emotionally trying evening, I realized I would need to approach my mother in private when I finally calmed down, in an effort to find truth and resolution. I could not move forward or come to a consensus without answers first, and my mother would need to take ownership for any truths that she had yet to share with me. Before we left the school, I planned to seek some answers as soon as we got home.

On the ride home, I held myself back from demanding answers from my mother then and there about what I had discovered. I did not want to make a scene in front of my family. As I thought more about it, I considered just contacting the records office. However, I finally realized I could not wait that long and function with such a cloud of confusion hovering over me.

Back home, I helped our kids to get ready for bed. I told my husband that I quickly had to run next door to my mom's house. On my way out, I scrutinized the paperwork one last time, before hiding it in my drawer.

I was soon knocking on my mother's door, full of emotion. My arm felt so heavy and detached from my body, knocking on that door. When my mother answered, I entered as usual, following her into the living room. However, I knew this would be no typical conversation. Needing answers sooner than later, I did not hesitate to start searching once we were seated.

Wasting no time, I began, "Mom, I got a certificate in the mail today and it seems as though there is a big mistake. The certificate says that I am adopted...."

My mom looked absolutely stunned, like a picture, frozen in time, except for her throat slowly tightening. My voice trailed off. In that moment, I was consumed by her body language, which after being around her for so long spoke volumes about a truth I did not want to believe.

"What do you have to say about this Mom? Why would they say this?"

The weight of her frozen frame sunk deeper into her chair. The emotion in her face soon followed, replaced by something cold and deflated. She sat there listlessly.

"It is out now" was all she could muster.

My heart hurt, sinking deeper into my chest as I spoke with her, until being stirred by a fire now growing inside of me. I was having difficulty controlling my emotions. This was a sensation I rarely felt.

I looked at her in disbelief and thundered, "What's out now?"

"Don't be angry with me. You... were kind of adopted." Without saying much, she had turned any remaining doubt I had into truth. This blow was even fiercer than my intensity.

Wounded, I asked, "What? Why didn't you tell me?"

"Lorna, I wanted to tell you, but your father swore me to secrecy. He never wanted you to know. I promised him I would never say anything."

"Who are my parents, mom? What happened?"

My mother's eyes locked onto mine as she shot out, "Your father is your father, but I am not your mother."

Her eyes then lowered as she looked away. Thoroughly confused, heated, and hurt, I had to know more. For a moment, I had great pity for this woman I had called mom for the past 30 years. The fire within me was now spreading uncontrollably. I sat there pensively as she began to recall my father's past behavior that led to all of this confusion I had stumbled upon.

"Your father had an affair with a married woman and she got pregnant. The woman he had the affair with was your biological mother. After she gave birth to you, your father wanted to take you and raise you with me. I had a few miscarriages, and the last time I lost my baby, I just felt it was not meant for me to have children. So when this happened, although I was really angry and hurt by your father's betrayal, I felt him having you was the answer to us finally having a family."

My scorching emotional state was hurting her. Her face was showing so. It was a story she most likely never intended to tell, but perhaps had always been searching for the right opening to. The situation slowly neutralized into a troubled reprieve that was felt in the room as she exhaled and continued.

"Lorna, your mother's husband did not want her to keep you. There was so much arguing and fighting between your father and her husband. Your mother's husband threatened to never allow your father to see you again if he did not provide some type of financial support."

Such news turned back up the heat. It was all so surreal. I was even more in a world of my own, not sure what was real and what was a lie anymore. This story that I was hearing for the first time was about my life. How could I have been kept in the dark for so long?

"My whole life is a lie!" I snapped back.

"Lorna," she rationalized, "if I had not taken you in, you would have been sent somewhere else and who knows if your father would have ever seen you again. Please, please Lorna, do not speak about this to anyone." That was surely an unbelievable request, having this cloud of confusion above me turn into one of unshakeable secrecy, about my adoption. To have it always hanging above me, with the expectation for me to just keep quiet and live with it.

"How dare she!" I thought.

That was all I could take that night. I could not process any more. My body took over, quickly moving into an evacuation mode. If this was not a dream, perhaps sleep would help?

In silence to myself, I wondered, "Who am I? Is what she is saying really true? Is my father really my father?" In 15 minutes, 30 years of my life story now has a different opening.

I rose from my chair and left a wounded woman still sunk in her living room. Not saying a word, I left, the door still open behind me. I walked away feeling mentally stunned, and each step I took felt like I was being lifted up into the air at the same time, a peddling of dissociative emotion.

Now, I had to pull myself together. Such a bombshell had just been dropped on me and I was now supposed to pretend like nothing happened? If I was to maintain secrecy, I first had to share this new beginning with my best friend, my husband.

Although I had known him since I was 14 years old, I could not figure out how I was going to explain something that I did not even fully understand myself. My new reality certainly impacted our entire shared history just as much. If anyone else was to know, it should be him.

I was frustrated with myself that I had already waited so long to say anything, wanting to first wait until I had learned more. This was a man who I had always shared all of my emotions with, yet telling him before now had seemed like too much.

Once I walked into our house, I had started to plan my outfit for the next day to distract myself. Sitting on my bed still numb, staring at the clothes in my closet, I took my certificate out of my drawer. I reread it, now with a new understanding.

My scrutiny of it continued, but now at the information itself with final acceptance, at my name, the day, and biological parents' names. As if on cue, I heard my husband entering the room. I quickly folded up the certificate and clutched it in my hand. My nerves were getting the best of me. I just wanted to feel the cool and calm I had always experienced in times of stress and crisis.

Would things ever feel normal again? I was supposed to be the one who could handle pressure and never let problems break me. For as long as I could remember, I had always been the strong, resilient one, the one who helped people through their problems and solved my own.

Unfortunately, this solution-oriented woman had run out of answers. My husband saw my unusual demeanor as I tried to pretend I was back in a state of calm like before today.

He asked, "What's the matter, you seem mad? You have been acting really strange all evening. You were not even paying attention during the open house. Don't think I did not notice it. Is there something you have to tell me?"

After a few moments of silence, I handed him the certificate and told him he should sit down before he read it. Looking very puzzled, he began reading it.

"What is this baby?"

Still full of emotion, I responded, "It is the paperwork sent to me instead of my birth certificate. I sent information just to get the paperwork needed for my passport. I am 31-years-old and this is what I find out from a piece of paper from someone who does not even know me!"

He looked as shocked as I did. "Did you talk to your mom about this? What did she say?"

I told him the whole story and her "it is out now" statement, which confirmed that what the paper stated was true, no turning back. I tried to refrain from making eye contact with him, as I knew that once our eyes met, he would then bear the full weight of what I was feeling. He would know my feelings of disbelief, anger, and betrayal.

He just held me in response, trying to give me comfort in the midst of dealing with his own shock. The embrace lasted for at least five minutes in silent consolation. It was a span of time where no words were spoken, two bodies once having a lifetime of knowing were now both coping with what felt like would be an eternity of unanswered questions.

I then got up and went to take a shower. With the water streaming down my face, I kept wondering what my biological mother was thinking about when she gave me up. "What did she look like? Did she ever wonder about me? Was she even still alive?" I went to sleep in a state of confusion. It was the lightest and most restless sleep I had ever had. Every time I looked at the ceiling, I could only see my new cloud of secrecy hanging over me, staring back.

-CHAPTER 3-
MOVING FORWARD

The next day I arose and attempted to resume my normal existence. Ironically, my usual schedule was not as ordinary and routine as it seemed. Although I had my 9 to 5 job, I never naturally fit into an easily-labeled box.

I was a teenage mother who went on to defy many statistics. I had graduated from high school and college, married my daughter's father, and went on to have another daughter. Furthermore, everyone saw me as pretty much having it all together, all of the time.

Yes, there was no denying that we struggled economically in those early years of marriage. Yet, although we were very young, we were still faring a lot better than many others in our situation. Early in our marriage, my husband had worked to support all of us: himself; a baby; and me, a full-time college student.

Back to my day at work, I found myself reflecting on the things I now knew to be true, while performing my duties on autopilot. I constantly found myself drifting off to a blank space in my mind. That day, I began to look at my Director, who had adopted children, in a completely different light. I had never had any connection to the adoption process except through watching him adopt his two children. Little did I know, I was connected to the process all along, more than I ever would have imagined. It was still hard to grasp just how much had changed so fast.

As the days went on, I walked around carrying out all of my roles and responsibilities, but there were new and unavoidable questions that materialized and then lingered. I still felt as if my life was not mine, as if I was living in someone else's reality. It was necessary that I remained strong, even if only on the outside, to prevent myself from crumbling. I began to question if what my husband often defined as my extreme resiliency had to do with my early upbringing.

Many of the people who knew me always seemed to think that I was very tough and could handle pressure, no matter how much. When my father suddenly became ill and passed away from a cerebral aneurism, while my mother was an absolute wreck, I handled everything with grace and tranquility. I spoke with the doctors about his aneurysm, planned the funeral, and made sure everything was in order, never falling apart as many others might have.

Having a determined focus in the face of stressful situations was the way I always was, not cold, but rather the type of personality that tries to remain composed to get whatever task at hand accomplished, to in turn spread hope and confidence to others around me. At work, I had a motto, "Don't let the problem blow your mind." They actually gave me my Employee of the Year award with that very message inscribed on it. I wondered if I had learned how to cope and deal with obstacles earlier on than I remembered. Was my separation something that allowed me to handle pain in a way that made me seem unbreakable?

My mind began to fill with questions that I wanted to ask my biological mother if I ever got the chance. I wanted to know if she ever thought about me, even after all these years of separation. How could she live with herself having given her child away? Do I have any brothers and sisters? Did she ever care during this whole ordeal? Did she ever love me? It was a growing list of questions for someone I might never even find. However, sometimes inquiring minds want to know, no matter the costs.

I soon began to consider trying to find my biological mother. Naturally inquisitive, these new questions got the best of me, so I soon threw myself into a full-throttle search for her. My relationship with my adoptive mother, to put it lightly, had become a bit strained, with no signs of immediate repair or many more answers coming from her without damaging what we had even further. It was torture not to know, while restraining my mounting unanswered questions about my origins.

One day I happened to be watching a television show where a woman said how nobody wants to begin a book on chapter two. I felt like that was the problem I was having. In a way, I did not have the full beginning of the story. As it turned out, the true first chapter had been, until recently, completely absent from the story of my life. There was a drive inside of me to peel apart these recently found pages, one answer at a time. However, one wrong move and I could negatively impact the potential I had in uncovering any more information.

Other thoughts and questions ranged from, is she still alive to what did she look like? I did not even know where she was living now. Furthermore, since I was born in another part of the world, how on earth would I ever find the information needed to search for her? Not everyone that is adopted decides to take the step of searching for his/her original birth parents. I came to realize this would be a major undertaking that would require much thought and guidance.

Yearning for answers, I had to start somewhere, so I contacted the Department of Vital Records in Europe and told them that although they sent me my adoption certificate, I wanted to get my actual birth certificate. I was then transferred through several more employees until I was told there was a separate process for acquiring such records.

I had to wait until I received some forms from them, at which point I could then request such information. I knew records were not available in some parts of the United States due to adoption laws and was thankful that the laws were different in England. I had actually finished the phone call unexpectedly hopeful. I might be able to get an old address or some piece of data that could help me find answers. This optimism helped to strengthen and slowly return me to who I once was, although things definitely felt different now.

I anxiously waited for the new information, while searching an adoption registry website where people who were looking for each other were listed. The internet was just starting to become popular for personal use, and I wanted to take advantage of all of the tools at my disposal. I also signed up for an adoption registry newsletter overseas called "AAA- NORCAP (Adults Affected by Adoption- National Organisation for Counseling Adoptees And Parents(UK) Currently called- BAFF British Association of Adoption and Fostering." Although small, these were steps moving me forward in my research.

The internet was becoming a growing part of my exploration, despite being somewhat challenging to navigate. It had allowed me to find the address for NORCAP and other details. Soon, the newsletter came, ironically, in another brown envelope. By this point, I began associating such envelopes with earthshattering information. Therefore, every time I saw one, it caused me to have a rapid heartbeat, even if it was just a nonthreatening and informative mailing.

This newsletter had a lot of information on searching for birth parents. Information included how to go about the process and prepare as the birth parent or adopted child, while also sharing the varied results. It felt as though I could not read enough about this process, as it helped me to feel connected to others who were most likely experiencing similar emotions as I was. These common bonds allowed me to accept my new reality further and become somewhat excited by its possibilities.

One section of the newsletter that was very powerful was titled reunion stories. The first one I read detailed a situation where a woman in her 20s located her biological mother and contacted her once she had gotten up the courage to take that next step. She wrote to her and asked to be a part of her life.

However, her biological mother indicated that she really did not want to start a bond with her at this point in her life. She had a new husband and two children who did not know anything about this part of her past. She was sorry, but she had closed that door and wanted to leave it shut.

Reading what I saw as an unhappy ending to the very first story I chose to read was disappointing and saddened me. I thought, "Suppose I find her, and this is what happens to me too?" If it did, I would feel rejected. Although I knew the story was meant to prepare readers for such a possibility, I could not accept that this was how it might end up. Despite any lingering doubt, I continued to pray that I would not have the same experience if I ever got that far.

Try as I might, after learning about my adoption, everything was no longer quite back to business as normal. However, to everyone around me, outside of Alonzo, it appeared to be life as usual. I continued to work, spend time on my local television show, and went to church as if nothing had changed, since that was my agreement, my cloud, mum's the word.

A quest for answers also helped me to obtain a bit more information delicately from my mother. She was happy by my agreement to secrecy. During this time, I asked her more questions about the process. I asked her if anyone else knew, because how could someone think she had a baby if she never looked pregnant. She told me she was not sure who knew, but believed one of my uncles in England might. As I waited for more information, I wondered which older family members knew; someone had to know she had not given birth to me, who knew that babies do not just appear out of thin air.

I also attributed how I maintained my typical persona during this time to connecting more deeply in my relationship with God. Reading stories about adoption and discovery were no replacement for God's guidance. I actually believed that I was being strengthened prior to being stretched. Had it not been for the grounding I was receiving from my increasing faith in God and the spiritual teachings of my church, I do not know how else I would have coped for so long.

My new knowledge especially impacted me several months prior to Mother's Day. As Mother's Day approached, I thought how this holiday would never be quite the same again. There were times when I became teary eyed and sometimes cried and said to myself, "life is so unbelievable," but I also felt as if things were happening for a reason. It was in those moments the most when I prayed, "Dear Lord, I know that this is not all happening by coincidence. Why did I find this out at this point in my life? Please help me make it through this journey and let me find my needle of a mother in this haystack of the world."

The quest for this needle was especially intimidating, as the whole world was the haystack. Although I felt I should have been told earlier, I wondered how I would have truly handled the news if I was told as a teenager. I felt that if they told me as a child, it would have probably been easier to accept. I returned again and again to wondering how I would have handled it during my adolescent stage of development. Would I have rebelled because of a lack of maturity and being shocked during a stage where teens are trying to solidify their identities?

All of these scenarios, played out in my mind, made me consider the things we think about, but rarely discuss, which are part of relationships between many mothers and their daughters. It is almost seen as a sin in many communities, especially those of color, to admit that the bond between you and your mother is not perfect. However, although my adoptive mother was always loving and good to me, I never had considered us to be a perfect match.

You might say we had just always been extremely different from each other. I had always attributed this to her being an older mother from a different era, somewhat old-fashioned in her ways. We would have little disputes and differences of opinion for as long as I could remember, oftentimes over the most trivial things.

My reliving the past made me remember, in particular, one day saying to my father, "Why is she always picking on me for every little thing?"

Now I know these types of complex relationships occur between biological mothers and daughters all of the time, but when I found out that I was adopted, I wondered if it was due to something more. Was there some type of incompatibility factor? How, if at all, did the lack of shared DNA influence things?

I could not rule out the potential impact that my birth situation and subsequent adoption may have had. The reality was I was the child of another woman. How did that preface her feelings toward me? I knew people who had been adopted and their relationships were great with their adoptive mothers, a bond so loving and close it just seemed meant to be. However, after some years of living with an unspoken distance between us, I questioned the origin of it more than ever now that this secret had been revealed to me. I concluded that these child-parent complexities could happen through a mixture of nature and nurture.

Thankfully, my husband Alonzo was so supportive during my wait for answers. There were many days filled with questions, and he would try everything to help me feel whole once more. I soon felt as if I was always waiting for information; the mailman became a sight for sore eyes.

The pieces of this puzzle, which would hopefully provide me with a fuller picture, were coming together too slowly for me to feel that there would ever be a final picture. During that time, a colleague mentioned how one cannot find peace until you find all of the pieces. As a result, I accepted that some unrest was inevitable. Each day without answers only reminded me of that once more.

With anxious difficulty, I waited for the package needed to request my original birth certificate information. I waited for three of the longest weeks of my life until it finally came. Once again, this information came in a brown envelope.

Several quick heart palpitations later, my search, for better or for worse, could finally continue. With hope, I quickly tore open the envelope and read the materials that instructed me how to fill out the forms to obtain the necessary information, items such as: name, date of birth, adopted parents information, date of adoption, and as much as I knew about the details. I then wrote down every word with careful intent and clarity that same day.

When everything was complete, I dropped to my knees and prayed as I sealed it, "Dear Lord, I am on a most-agonizing journey toward truth. Help me through this process. This is so much to handle at this stage in my life. Please give me the answers I need to find who my mother is. Please give me the answers I need to find out who I am and what life is supposed to be now."

I also asked the Lord to allow this request to lead me to the truth and my biological mother. I had already made copies of all of the information and addressed the envelope. In truth, I did not think I had ever filled out any forms so quickly before. They were in the mail the very next day as the waiting process then began all over again.

With more progress made, I began to put the name listed as my biological mother on the adoption certificate into various internet search engines and websites: Margaret Brown. I still did not know if she was living, and the information I was coming up with was just as inconclusive. The adoption certificate was proving not as helpful as I had hoped it would be.

What was perplexing was that it listed her last name as Brown. Strangely, that was my maiden name. My search was actually producing only more questions than answers. As I looked for new mail each day, waiting for more information to come, I wondered what I would find out and if it would even prove to be any more helpful than what I already knew.

Although the wait seemed like forever, one day the information finally came. Once again, my heart started pounding at the sight of another envelope waiting outside of my door. I sat down to brace myself as I read over its contents after pulling out the four pieces of paper inside. I saw the title, birth certificate! I saw my mother's name and age and her husband's name. According to the certificate, it appeared my biological mother had me when she was 21 years old. She may still be young enough to be alive! This provided me with even more faith for the future. One of the things that also jumped out to me was that we shared the same birthday.

When I saw January 16, I thought to myself, "Oh my Lord, God made sure that she could not completely forget about me! Every time she has a birthday, I also have a birthday."

This was a stunning and noteworthy find for me. How amazing it was that we shared the same birthday. Perhaps I was not forgotten after all! That was by far the most-exciting piece of the documentation for me.

Another piece of information only provided me with more confusion than answers. I had clearly been told that my dad was my biological father. However, this new document had listed my biological mother's husband as my dad instead. Had my mother not told me the full truth? Did she still have secrets left concealed?

Once again, I thought to myself, "What is going on?"

After weighing her word against what I was reading, I gave my mother the benefit of the doubt when she had told me that the father I had always known was my biological one. I looked a lot like him and we had a lot of similarities, at least so I had thought. Once again, it felt like some strangers were providing me with documents that caused me to wonder what was true and what was an oversight.

Ironically, because I looked so much like my father, I never thought much about the fact that I did not really resemble my mother. However, there were a few specific traits that people often attributed to her. They would say things like, "you have hair just like your mother's family."

It is interesting how heredity becomes so important when you add in the unknowns of adoption. The identity factor was very intriguing. As someone who had always been fascinated with genes, biology, and sociology, it caused me to think about what I was made of and where one's characteristics originate.

When you do not know where you came from, your mind runs awry. You cannot help it. Various fantasies take over where your long-lost relatives are rich or famous and beautiful. With so many questions, I would come up with amazing possibilities while I awaited the truths. One such fleeting thought that ran through my mind even came after seeing an interview on television from London with Melanie Brown, from the band The Spice Girls. I fancifully wondered, since having the same last name as her and also being from London, "Maybe I am related to her?"

However, in truth, I knew better than that, but sometimes you think these strange or romanticized thoughts in an attempt to ease the ache of uncertainty. Back to reality, I thought about the fact that it did not matter. What my biological mother did or did not have was unimportant, as I did not want anything from her in return for me ever finding her beyond her acceptance; I just wanted to get to know her and learn why she decided that she could not keep me. This had become my biggest question I needed to have answered.

Included in the paperwork was a letter that said I could get the details of the adoption, but I would first need to see an adoption counselor, someone locally who had been trained in helping adoptees work through such intricacies. I guess they felt it was necessary to have someone that could help you process and review this information in a safe and knowledgeable environment.

Once I followed-up on this letter and received the paperwork detailing available counselors, I selected one from the list.

The information indicated that they would send me their contact information after I submitted the processing fee. This was supposed to cover the processing of the paperwork, and the $150.00 counselor's fee would be paid when we met. I could then receive the information I wanted. It would only be sent directly to the counselor, not to me. I was so excited because I just wanted some form of an address for my birth mother, even if it was from 30 years ago.

As I debated taking this next step, I continued to use the internet and phone directory to search for the name listed on the original adoption certificate. I also sent a simple and nondescript letter to the first address on the birth certificate; my letter read: My name is Lorna and I am trying to locate Margaret. She is a relative who I am trying to find. Please respond if you know her or if you are her.

In truth, I doubted she still lived there. I did not expect much of a response back, as people generally have moved after such a long period of time. Although I did not hear anything even after a couple of weeks, at least the letter was never returned. I then contacted the adoption office and indicated I was willing to move forward. Taking this initiative, I could not believe things were finally moving closer to what I hoped would be an ideal resolution. Would I ever get to know Margaret? I prayed I would.

-CHAPTER 4-
TRUTH CLARIFIED

Soon, the papers came, listing the names of the adoption counselors. I began to anxiously make some phone calls. Since this was a European organization, they had counselors spread throughout the country. As a result, not many of them were located nearby, causing me some difficulty in successfully locating and connecting with someone quickly.

This was rather disappointing, as working in the human services field I had a certain expectation on how counselors and professionals should respond to those in need of assistance. Such expectations, like promptly returning calls, were not necessarily demanding either. Rather, they were just expectations I had felt every individual who was in need deserved.

In the beginning, I tried several times to reach the closest counselor. Although I called numerous times and left messages, I received no response. Having no returned calls made me frustrated and even wonder if this was a sign that I should not go any further. However, I could not accept getting so close, only to give up because the person that was supposed to help me was actually preventing me from getting the information I needed. This simply would not do.

Still desiring to make progress, I contacted the British adoption counseling department to complain about how this one counselor handled his business, or in my case, apparently did nothing to even try. Although it may have just been part of the daily grind for him, with my name on some eventual to-do list, it felt like a matter of life and death for me that was becoming increasingly wearisome.

The adoption counseling department indicated they had only worked with him a few times and had not received any feedback, negative or otherwise. I asked them what criteria and credentials someone would need if I were to be proactive and find my own counselor to have him/her join as part of their network. This was because, prior to my call to them, I had contacted some people from my professional network, having indicated I was searching for someone specializing in adoption counseling or search-related matters. However, they also assumed I was searching for this for a client, as I never told them anything different. Each day the number of individuals I interacted with who I did not tell my secret to grew, as my cloud of secrecy still remained above me.

Although not part of their network, the adoption counseling department provided me with the name of a West Hartford counselor Karen Caffrey, LPC, JD, who specialized in adults dealing with adoption. However, they informed me that adding her to their network could take over three months, time that I did not have. Just to talk to someone about my situation, I called her and spoke to her over the phone anonymously, as I carefully explained my circumstances.

Although she was not a part of the network, she said she would be willing to assist me. She could not believe I was able to get all of the adoption information that I had, as she explained how adoption records are often sealed. She was very sympathetic and understanding for someone who was just talking to a stranger. She also said that with a situation like this, she would highly recommend some adoption counseling. In the end, I felt better just speaking with her and being on the receiving end of her caring demeanor. Such a helpful conversation had given me a great sense of relief and motivation to continue moving forward.

Then, experiencing quite the opposite reception, I finally connected with the counselor who was originally listed as a part of the European network. He somewhat indifferently provided me with an appointment. Even after his delay in getting back to me, he made me wait over two weeks to see him, reiterating to me the associated fee.

He seemed to be placing higher importance on my money than on my needs. I held back every urge in my body to point out how he was coming across over the phone. In the end, I figured, his two weeks were shorter than the three months to get the other counselor into the network. Maybe he would be more pleasant in person?

Although I did not have the best introduction to him initially, as he seemed so cold, I had to focus on the fact that this was an unavoidable step in the process. I had bigger things to be concerned about. As my appointment approached, Alonzo asked me if I would like him to go with me. After some consideration, I decided that I would like to go alone, although I asked him to keep his cell phone on in case I for any reason needed to reach him. With my plans for the day solidifying in my head, the day of my meeting could not come soon enough.

As planned, I went to work on the day of my appointment. He could not see me until 3:00 pm. My stomach was full of butterflies that day, but excited at the same time. It was hard to concentrate, as I my mind ran through how my meeting might go and what I could find out. Although I had received directions, I was not familiar with the rather rural area he was located in. To be safe, I anxiously left at 1:30 pm, as I did not want to be late, and I knew it would take at least 45 minutes to get there. The drive was a blur of scenery, but its details were lost to me as my mind still raced around the meeting and what might come out of it.

Before my mind completely carried me away, I finally

arrived at the building after taking a wrong turn and getting off at a wrong exit. Luckily, I did find my way back and ended up at a very small and ordinary office complex. Would this unassuming building and what happened inside it bring me the answers I needed? My hand knocked on the office door with nervous excitement, but there was no answer, so I figured that he must be in session with someone else.

During the wait, I felt my chances for a positive meeting dwindle as it felt more and more like he was standing me up. My positive emotions put up a fight to not be altered. Waiting is hard enough, never mind when the wait hinges on finding your birth parent/s.

The whole time, I just kept saying to myself, "All of this is going to be a blessing to you Lorna. Just hang in there. You have waited this long. You can make it a little longer."

As the minutes ticked on, my mind would shift to, if he shows up, I am going to let him have it, but then I would check myself, remembering that he had valuable information I needed and this was not the moment to rock the boat and let my emotions get the best of me.

My assumption that he was in another meeting ended up being false. He actually was never there to begin with. In reality, he ended up arriving 35 minutes late. Regardless, when he finally showed up, I was so happy just to see him, to know this meeting would actually take place. I went into his office with him and sat down, while restraining my emotions to remain cordial. He started by stating that it was important that I understood the impact of this information and how part of his job was to make sure I could handle the process.

As I listened to him very intently, I kept thinking, "Okay, I get this. I know all of that. Please hurry up and get to the good stuff!"

I assumed that he had already read the contents and could provide me with some additional guidance on how to go about any next steps once our meeting concluded, not just regurgitate to me what I already knew.

"Where's the payment?" He actually asked me for it upfront, which really solidified for me his poor social work skills in dealing with clients like me. As many social services workers would agree, there is more than just money involved when working with human lives.

We had already agreed over the phone how he needed to be paid. More and more of this conversation had already taken place already. What did he expect, that I would bolt out of the room after he gave me the information? Did he realize that I was yearning to learn some very critical information about my life and would not have come here, meeting with him, if I was not serious? It verified how he was more worried about being paid than doing what he was paid to do, help people.

He went on to read me a standard statement about the information being confidential and wanted to make sure I realized that this person may or may not be receptive to hearing from me. Then, he handed me the file, which contained a few pieces of paper from the adoption counseling department. It was finally in my trembling hands! The full and accurate name of my biological mother and the key pieces of paperwork that outlined how the adoption transpired would not be a mystery any longer.

Upon opening, I learned that my mother was married and that the baby was not her husband's. This was apparently why the baby, me, was being placed up for adoption. There was additional information that was confusing, stating how she was going to place the baby with her uncle and aunt. Strangely, the name listed on the records as her uncle was who I had always known to be my father.

I asked him if the information on these records was accurate. He said it was. Furthermore, I asked him to tell me if I could contact the agency to ask for additional information. He thought I might be able to, but could not make any guarantees. Although I was so happy to get this information, for all of the questions that were answered, again new ones arose. I guess I had more fact-finding to do.

As I read through the paperwork, I saw that I had at least two sisters, knowledge that made me very excited! It was piece of my life that I had never experienced before, growing up as an only child. In the midst of my draining journey, a void was now being filled. I had at least two sisters after all! Sisterly experiences might be within my grasp. Although I did not know who they were, at least I had siblings.

However, the information, although exciting, was also dated. Going into this meeting, I had hoped I would have been provided with some current information, such as an address or something additional to help me locate her. I was not that fortunate.

I asked him if he knew of any places where one might get assistance with searching, and he told me AAA-NORCAP, which I was already aware of. He then basically indicated how our time was up and there was nothing else he could do. I signed the necessary forms, still in a mixture of emotions. Internally, I kept reminding myself how this meeting had to happen if I were to make progress.

As I signed the forms, I thought, "If only he had been more prepared and came into the meeting with a feeling of what I was going through."

Before I left, I thanked him and reminded him that people come to him in a very sensitive and fragile state when they request this information and how it is important to treat them with interest, dignity, and respect. As politely as possible, I noted how this is not just another business transaction. I then stepped out of his office, delightedly armed with my newfound information. I soon elatedly called my husband to tell him what I had learned.

On the drive home, I reflected to myself, "He definitely was not very empathetic, nor all that helpful during our session," and although it was information that I was thrilled to have, I left feeling as if I could have benefited from a lot more clarification. However, what was important was that I now had what I needed to move ahead with my research. There would be no need for me to ever meet with him again I reminded myself, whenever negative thoughts resurfaced.

Having received this new information concerning my adoption, I now struggled with where the truth lied. On one hand, this information was apparently the truth. On the other, what my mom told me, she also claimed to be the truth.

Was my mother covering up more than she had let on? Did she only give me half of the story? I thought back on the limited number of baby pictures of me before the age of three. It never seemed odd to me; we had moved from Europe to the United States and simply did not take a lot of pictures until we finally purchased a camera when I was about seven. It was not like I had a house filled with brothers and sisters to compare my amount of pictures with. Some families would rather just capture moments in their minds.

In trying to remember all of the pictures, there was one that vividly came to me. It looked as if I was about one year old, no big deal. Yet, after a life-changing experience like this, I guess I had begun to question all of the things that previously seemed typical. I remembered how it looked like the photo had been taken from a distance, almost as if from across the street. This never occurred to me as unusual, but rather just one of many ways to take a picture. I was sitting on the front lawn in a pretty dress and beautiful bonnet. Did my mother and father take it without my biological mother even knowing about this potential act of spying or vice versa? I continued to feel as if I needed to know how long I had lived with my biological mom.

It was not long after I got home from my meeting with the counselor that I knew I had to go to my mother's house to try to pull more answers from her. Although I was nervous about asking her more questions, I had no choice, as I couldn't ask my father since he died of an aneurysm in 1990. She seemed to be somewhat uncomfortable talking about the topic regardless of what question I posed. Remembering back to previous conversations with her, she would often say she could not remember details, details that I thought she still should be able to. She could not have been that forgetful. Maybe she had blocked them out of her mind? Perhaps she had never experienced them firsthand?

During a previous visit, I had asked her, "Do you remember how old I was when I came to live with you?"

She responded, "I believe you were a few months old."

I also inquired of her, "Was I a fussy child?"

To which she replied, "No, not really, you just had frequent colds."

What I really wanted to know was if I appeared to be longing for my biological mother by crying a lot, causing sicknesses from the detachment I felt. I needed to find out the whole truth. The new paperwork provided me with "my new truth," another here-we-go-again, more secrets and revelations.

Knowing that these unanswered questions would not answer themselves, I summoned the courage for the uncomfortable conversation that might follow. I needed to know more. Not one to sit still, I was off again to my mother's house. When I arrived, I delicately told her that I had received more paperwork, and I wondered if she could help explain its contents to me.

I informed her how the documentation revealed that my birth… (although I had started to say my birth mother, I knew doing so would have hurt her, so I stopped myself short and called her by name) Margaret had an affair with a man during a separation from her husband and became pregnant. As a result, she wanted to give the baby up for adoption to live with an uncle who was listed with my father's/her husband's name. I asked her why this was.

She told me how this was untrue and was just what they had told the agency, as it was less embarrassing that way. Although this added to my mother's history of secrecy and being guarded, it allowed me to breathe a sigh of relief that my story did not have to become any more complicated. There was a lot of shame involved with the whole affair and resulting pregnancy. By saying the baby was going to a family member, it apparently made things better, at least in my parents' eyes.

The rest of our visit was actually quite cordial, never becoming confrontational or too uncomfortable. I left taking her responses at around 90% honesty, which was good enough for me. I wanted to believe at this point, but also not make my mother so overwhelmed that she refused to answer more questions I might come up with in the future.

Since "it" was out now, there really should have been no reason to lie about anything. Who would it benefit at this point? With all that had happened, I felt like I had to stay on top of the truth. I quickly moved from a questioning to a grateful attitude toward this newly-obtained information.

I thanked God for what he had helped me to uncover. I had a full name for my birth mother, her ex-husband's name, and two sisters, not to mention information on Margaret's ethnicity and education. My mind filled with thoughts of exciting possibilities to come.

The documents also indicated that Margaret was attractive and intelligent. I thought for them to document both of those things, these qualities must have been overtly apparent at the time. This was the most information I had to date. I felt like a little kid, proud to hear her mother be called pretty and smart!

A very important piece that I knew would help me during my search was her actual last name. The new paperwork revealed a different name than the one on the initial certificate. Furthermore, it was much less common. I thanked God for that as well!

As it turned out, the name that was initially listed was her maiden name, the same as my own, which was a much more common name and had not helped me to narrow down my search at all. Instead, her less-common last name helped me start to search for a needle in a smaller haystack, although I still believed that haystack to be all of the way across the pond.

From the time I had found out about my adoption and focused my energies into finding out more answers to the receipt of this paperwork, I had continued to go through my day-to-day existence as best as I could, along with working, church, and family time. It was amazing the range of emotions I had felt in such a short amount of time. I had some close friends, family, and in-laws that I could normally talk with.

However, I could not share the discovery of my life with them. This agreement was extremely challenging for me, because I felt like I was being dishonest by not sharing. Faithfully, I still had to honor my mother's request, even at my own discomfort. Not sharing was frustrating, but there seemed to be no alternative.

I continued to reread the information I had received as I tried to figure out how I could begin to locate her, all the while praying that she was still alive. When Alonzo got home that evening, after I had received my paperwork, he looked it over and also pondered the information. He too questioned how the paperwork stated that my biological father was not the father that I had known, which he was relieved to know was not true.

I began to tell him in detail how impersonal the whole process was with the counselor, my body reliving the same emotions I had felt during the appointment as I told him. Reflecting back made me know then and there that I was going to make sure that the adoption counseling department knew how he had handled my case for future referrals. There was no reason why he should continue on in this capacity with no reviews to his name. If for any reason he was more professional than what I had experienced, let his future reviews prevail over mine.

During our conversation, I posed a question to Alonzo, "If I was in there behaving more hysterical, would he have been more caring or sensitive?" I doubted it.

I have always felt the need to be an advocate, not just for my-self, but for others as well. Such insensitivity needed to be reported. I went on to contact the department and share the unsatisfying details of our meeting and his delay in returning my phone calls.

Similar to what I said to him, I also told them that people are in such an emotional place during the search process, so their counselors should at least show some empathy and demonstrate some amount of care and concern. The experience made me realize just how important these counselors actually are for adopters, adoptees and their families. It also made me more appreciative for how I treated any of the clients who contacted me.

The next few pages are images that are significant to the author's journey.

What images in your life are meaningful and would tell your story?

Public Health Department

* Division No....................

IMMUNISATION RECORD OF

Name............ ~~LORNA BROWN~~

born on.........16../............/...........

Address (1)..........~~................~~

Subsequent Addresses :

(2)...46 Edelvin St SW...

(3)...106 Plengall Rd...

(4)..................

P.5288

CERTIFIED COPY OF AN ENTRY IN THE
RECORDS OF THE GENERAL REGISTER OFFICE

Given at the GENERAL REGISTER OFFICE,
SOMERSET HOUSE, LONDON

Levi Brown
106 Glensall Road

Sixteenth January 1986

BY AIR MAIL
par avion
Royal Mail

BY AIR MAIL
PAR AVION

Lorna at 3 years old, one of her earliest pictures.

THREE FROM ONE
A PORTRAIT OF
OUR MOTHER

The Catalyst - The quest for this document started
the chain of events.

-CHAPTER 5-
FAITHFUL PURSUIT

Now knowing Margaret's actual last name, the next day I started plugging it into every website possible in a quest for more answers. Although this meticulous process of combing the internet for clues did not provide me with any direct matches, I did find some individuals with her same married surname. I was once again so thankful for that distinctive last name. If it really had been Brown, I would have never been able to distinguish her from the millions of listings for Margaret Brown I had come across.

Instead, I could experience an adrenaline rush every time I found someone with this same last name. Unfortunately, these names were spread all over the world. If anything, at least the process was making me feel as if it would not be so impossible to find her after all.

After a few days, I whittled my search down to three phone numbers, hoping by fate I stumbled across a connection that would lead me in the right direction. I thought about what I would say to the person on the other end. How could I come across in a way that they were not turned off by my phone call, while maintaining a degree of secrecy and anonymity? I had to think about maintaining Margaret's confidentiality too, just in case these numbers led me to talking with other family members who did not know the truth to the extent I now knew, a truth I had almost never found out myself.

In preparation, I rehearsed in my mind what I would tell them if I successfully reached someone. I would make sure not to let on completely why I was calling, inquiring about Margaret. Not knowing Margaret beyond her name and what my mother told me, I also did not know who else knew about me in her family or who else made up her immediate and extended relations.

All of the work I had put in leading up to this point was now hinging on the success I had during these next three phone calls, or else it was back to the drawing board. While I had learned so much about the start of my life, which I still had a hard time comprehending how it had become so heavily rewritten, I knew every decision I made needed to be cautious so I could fulfill my hopeful prayer of contacting her. If she was still alive, I wanted her to receive me knowing I had the best intentions every step of the way.

With a deep breath, I began to call these long-distance numbers; the first in England. I dialed the numbers listed on the website, followed by the numbers on my calling card, then anxiously awaited a dial tone. The first call started out with an English ringtone, which was actually quite different than the way the phone rings in the United States. This ring came through loud and clear. Action was taking place! My body was filling with hope until I heard the operator message stating the number was no longer in service. My heart had been in my throat as I dialed, but this feeling of optimism was quickly decreasing. There were only two numbers left now.

The next number was also in England. I was nervous because I did not want to reach her husband, which would potentially reopen more old wounds based on what I had heard concerning their relationship. I started to dial it. My heart shot back up inside my throat once I heard a man's voice pickup on the other end. I asked for Margaret. Unfortunately, he stated that

I had the wrong number. I told him that I was an out-of-town relative and asked if he was familiar with her or any of her family, but was met with no success. Once again, I was left disenchanted. I returned to staring hopefully at last of the names and the phone numbers I had found, trying to use deductive reasoning and hoping that the third time would in fact be the charm.

I prayed, "Lord, please help me to have picked the right name so I can find out if she is alive and if so, where she is."

The last number I contacted was in Jamaica. I let the phone ring until I heard a woman's voice answer my call.

"Hello… hello," I greeted, "I wonder if you could assist me… I am trying to reach Margaret… I am a relative from the United States trying to reach her."

She replied, "Who are you looking for? Margaret…? Well, I know her, but she does not live here. Who are you again?"

Could it be? Does she know the Margaret I am looking for? I tried to maintain my composure as my body wanted to get up and celebrate. At this point, I then tried to tactfully explain how I was a relative who was trying to reach her. I indicated I was not sure where she or her family now lived.

She paused for a minute and then gave a strange sigh, before revealing, "I was her sister-in-law, and she lives in England."

This simple bit of information made me absolutely ecstatic! I could not believe I had just found my first real hope that she was still alive. The haystack was now only the size of England, instead of the whole world! I tried to lessen my bubbling over excitement to remain inconspicuous.

She continued, "What is your name?"

"Lorna," I truthfully replied.

She added, "Her daughters, my nieces, live in England."

I said, "Do you mean Sharon and Lorna?"

She corrected me, "You mean Sharon and Linda."

The paperwork had indicated that the child born ten months after me had the same first name, Lorna, which I had found to be an odd decision at the time. However, apparently this was not the case, but rather another mistake in the paperwork that was supposedly the truth.

She went on, "You are Lorna..."

This otherwise obvious statement led me to believe that she knew who I was and about the entire situation. She had a very intrigued tone during the remainder of the conversation. Why would she give out this information, especially the way she clarified who I was? She asked where I lived. I told her in the United States.

Moving the conversation back to Margaret, I asked her if she had a phone number or address, but she said that she had not talked to her or her nieces for quite some time. Even without the direct answer I had wanted, calling these numbers to result in such success definitely moved me further along. In the end, I thanked her for her time and for all of the information she had the ability to give to me. Thank God for this third number I had called!

I used the sound of the phone being hung-up to help me to muffle my shriek of excitement. Unfortunately, I could not explain to almost anyone why I was so incredibly excited without having to tell them the truth. I was home alone with the kids, so having to hide such a level of overwhelming jubilation was challenging. Needless to say, they had seen their mother exhibit some very different and unexplainable emotions lately.

To think, I finally made contact with someone who knew of "my new, yet old family." Her apparent interest made me really believe that she knew about me and some aspect of the adoption as well. Perhaps I am more than just a memory that everyone has since forgotten. I could not get over the fact of how amazing it was that I only had to make several calls, out of the hundreds of names I reviewed, to connect with a real lead. Technology helped me tremendously during this process, making me grateful for computers and this new search tool, the internet, too.

Believing Margaret to still be alive, and others to also know who I was, I began to think about what that must have been like for her to give me up. It was hard for me to imagine what it must have been like to have a sister-in-law and other family members know you had become pregnant by another man, only to then have to give the baby away. The sense of intrigue in this relative's voice made me feel her disclosure was also helping her in the process. It was as if my call was also giving her a sense of satisfaction to help me connect with Margaret, as if she said, "Margaret, you thought this was done years ago - well, guess what?"

Still overwhelmed by excitement, I had to tell my husband. I called Alonzo immediately on his cell phone and was so excited that I realized I was rambling almost incoherently.

He asked, in an effort to gain clarification, "You found your mother?"

I said, "No, but I found out she lives in England and she was alive at least as of a few years ago."

As he was on his way home, we agreed that we would continue the conversation once he arrived. We were so elated when he came home as we reminisced on everything that had transpired and how amazing this whole process had been during such a short amount of time. To actually have someone answer one of the few numbers I had selected and share that they knew Margaret was a great sign that we were moving in the right direction and this whole search was meant to endure. I felt so light the whole evening that it felt like my feet were off the ground.

The next day, I feverishly began searching the internet for Margaret and my sisters' names in England. Although results came slowly, I remained persistent. I also searched using Margaret's husband's name as well. As fate would have it, after a couple of weeks of trying, I received a new NORCAP newsletter that had information on their own search and registry services. I poured over this information and to see if there were any costs attached. I had to consider any and all options carefully, since the last person that helped me as a professional had not seemed in it because he cared. Yet, I recognized that a negative interaction again would be better than no communication at all.

I contemplated the various names as I prayed, "Lord, please guide me to select the right person to help me with my search."

I felt in my spirit that I was then directed to a woman on the list named Faith. I took a deep breath before I called her to discuss what I was looking for. She explained, in her proper British accent, how she worked professionally for a bank, but was also supporting adoptees in their search process because it was what she loved to do. It was refreshing to talk to someone who sounded like she genuinely cared about the people she worked with.

She reiterated upfront similar knowledge I already had going into the conversation, such as how her help may not provide me with the results I desired. Sometimes she located people and other times she did not, so there would be no guarantees. She also reminded me that there were also times when the person found may or may not respond, even if they are located and attempts at contact are made.

I went on to ask her how she conducted the searches, since I was not sure where she lived and had already searched some directories and phone information myself, coming up with several individuals with that same surname. However, none of them had the same first and last name in combination.

She explained, "I can't guarantee, but I will search through some databases I have worked with."

I replied inquisitively, "How much do you charge?"

To my surprise, she indicated that she did this for free. She was adopted herself and wanted to help others find their birth families as well. What a blessing!

I anxiously provided her with everything I had come up with so far to make her search easier, specifying names, dates, past known addresses, and the recent phone calls I had made. She complimented me on what she thought was already an impressive amount of research and was especially surprised that I had found out so much from such a far-away distance. Lastly, she indicated that it would take her a few weeks at the least, and if she located anything or not she would be getting back to me.

More than grateful, I mentioned, "You know, your name is a part of why I have faith in you."

She just laughed and told me to try to keep my patience while I waited to hear back from her. It was hard to contain my delight. This next step taken appeared to be continuing my search in the right direction. It was in the hands of God now. If Margaret was to be found, I was confident that Faith would find her. All I needed was an address. In terms of Margaret's husband, I knew that she was no longer with him, so I did not want to go that route.

Instead, my mind wandered in many other directions as I began to consider how this could end. Would my story resemble the first one I read about in NORCAP's search and reunion stories? Would she find a current address that actually allowed me to send a letter? I was so mixed with emotions that this waiting period made me feel like my life was temporarily in limbo. My husband was also experiencing these same emotions as he traveled on this journey of the unknown with me. My life was once again a big waiting game as I struggled to put as much energy and thought into my daily routine as I was putting into thinking about Faith's search.

As this process was underway, one day while I was at work, a colleague began to share his story about his wife finding her father, the father that she had never known. Although she was not adopted, she had been raised by her aunt and had not been told much about her father. He began to share the stress and the excitement of them having their first telephone conversation. Happily, he also shared that his wife just found out that she has three sisters after all of these years and that she is the only one that has children.

He then went on to tell me that they wanted to go and meet them, but there existed some uneasiness, as his wife's father's wife and daughters may not know about her. I could not believe what I was hearing from this colleague and good friend of mine, this person who had no inkling that he was sharing a story that resonated with my own life in a way that he might never know. I felt like the Lord was giving me another sign that miracles happen: a sign that these situations are more common than I thought. I wanted to share with him how I was walking a similar journey, but I could not. I was remaining largely positive despite my cloud above me.

Several restless days later, I was at work late one day, when the phone rang.

I heard a voice on the other end, "Hello, may I speak with Lorna Little?"

I responded intrigued, "This is Lorna."

Once I picked up on the British accent, I thought it might be Faith, "Hello, Lorna, this is Faith. How are you?"

My heart was once again racing a mile a minute toward what would hopefully be good news and more answers. I was so thankful to receive her call, even though I had no idea of its result. To think, I had been planning to go home early that day, but I ended up working later than originally planned. It was again by fate that she happened to call me now. We were in different time zones, but still found a way to connect.

She said "Well, I want to let you know I have searched several directories and came up with a few listings."

Furthermore, she revealed she had found a Linda. She went on to provide me with Linda's full name and phone number. There was also a Sharon Agarwal, which she had an address and phone number for, and also a Jamie Agarwal. The final information was for M. Agarwal, who did not list his/her full name, only first initial and address, as her number was unlisted. Was this

Margaret? Did she not want to be found? Either way, the joy I had in learning this information overpowered any such doubts at the moment.

She explained how they were all located in the same area in South London and hoped this information helped me. Their proximity must be more than coincidence! I struggled to contain my excitement, until I couldn't any longer. My eyes started watering as I told her how she was an angel sent from heaven and how the work she was doing was truly a blessing to all of us in similar situations. I thanked her profusely and then we ended our call. Once more, I now had to try to compose myself so my excitement did not draw any suspicion or tough questions.

I quickly wrapped up the work I was engaged in and took with me the list I had transcribed, full of new leads, with names, addresses, and phone numbers! I felt as though my body was making one big grin as I went down the elevator to go home. I knew two of the names had to be my sisters, but I could not contact them, as they may not even know I existed. Instead, I decided on the drive home that I would send a letter to the newfound address for M.A. and see what happens. I prayed this abbreviation stood for Margaret and that she received me well.

That evening, I sat with my kids and husband at the dinner table in a great mood, which I had come to terms with how it was once again impossible to hide.

Always attentive, my oldest daughter, Alicia, commented, "You are in a really good mood today."

I said as nondescript as possible, not to give anything away, "I had a great day."

While we ate, I looked at my family and wondered when and how I would ever tell them about this? After supper, I sat down to write the letter, which was surprisingly not as difficult as it could have been, as by this point I had rehearsed its contents in my head so many times. All of the emotions my heart contained easily poured forth, in hopes for a response, onto the page.

In the end, I kept it simple. I added a picture of myself from high school and made sure the letter was free from as little blame as possible. I actually typed it at the computer and saved a copy. I had my husband read it at least five times that night to make sure it was perfect and set the right tone for a good first impression. Each time, he reassured me it was fine. We held hands and prayed prior to me sealing yet another envelope, as I planned on dropping it in the mail the next morning. Prior to, I had gone to get extra postage to ensure the air-mail postage was sufficient.

The next morning came, and the letter was mailed. It was now on its way to London! During yet another time of waiting in my life, I wondered what I would do if she did not respond. Would I then contact my sisters?

I also wondered to myself if the other name on the list was related to my biological mom's husband. I reminded myself again, I wanted to contact him as a last resort. I did not need to reopen any old wounds if there were any, especially upon concluding that they were not still together based on how her sister-in-law clarified how she was her ex-sister-in-law. In the end, I decided that it was simply too early to have such thoughts, and I did not know what their relationship was like. It was a good thing I was now so used to waiting.

-CHAPTER 6-
CATCHING UP

As I waited, I kept myself sane by remembering all of the amazing facts I had discovered in such a short time. Margaret and I both shared the same birth date, so I felt she could not forget me, even if she had tried to.

Throughout my journey of discoveries, starting with learning I had been adopted, there had been many situations that may have seemed like coincidences. However, I believed them to be more clearly God moments that I liked to call "ordaincidents."

About three weeks after I sent my letter, I came across a movie partway through on Showtime called "Secrets & Lies," starring Brenda Blethyn and Marianne Jean-Baptiste. The amazing thing about this movie was that it is set in England and the main character actually finds out she is adopted upon the death of a parent. Watching her emotional response once she finds out about her secret adoption, I could relate to everything she was experiencing on the screen.

As it turned out, the birth mother's family is white. In the movie, because she is black, she has no idea she had any white lineage. However, this family also had another layer of issues to add to the situation. The socioeconomic differences between the families were also something to think about that I had never considered before now. What if Margaret came from another social class? Do differences like this change how a birth parent accepts his/her child?

What also stuck out in my mind, which I had never fully thought through, was witnessing the dynamics between the siblings. When the siblings were initially so resistant to this new, unknown sister, it made me think, "What if this happens to me when my sisters hear that I exist, if they do not already know, and feel a similar way?"

I fought back tears throughout watching the part of the movie I had come across, because the topic and the setting felt so real and gave me both new hopes and doubts to ponder. Why did this movie happen to be airing now? Was it put there just for my viewing as I waited for a response from who I hoped to be Margaret?

My husband also noticed these incredible "occurrences." The different leads and situations that were coming into my life to help me find and remind me of my needle in a haystack were simply incredible and at times felt too good to be true. I felt blessed.

Unsuspecting, one day shortly thereafter, I went to our mailbox and there was an air-mail letter from M. Agarwal! This could not be a letter from my Margaret, my needle, could it? The parcel felt so light, and it was in an air-mail envelope, not like all of my other earth-shattering mail that had arrived in brown envelopes. It was different, but felt so right.

Would it open or close a door to my past? I really felt it was from her before even opening it, even though I just had the first initial of her first name. I walked the package quickly into the bedroom. What was she going to say? Would it resemble any of the reunion stories I read? If it was her, would she want anything to do with me after so many years? I felt hot and tingly all over. There was emotion flooding through me in waves.

Once the bedroom door was shut, I tore open the letter and started to read it. It began with, "Hello my dearest Lorna." I continued anxiously reading word after word. It was from Margaret! She actually indicated that she knew that I would find her eventually, for the past ten years now. For her, she just had a feeling that had finally come true through my letter to her attention. She also commented on the high school yearbook picture I had sent to her. To my surprise, she said that it was exactly how she envisioned I would look!

I could not believe it; after so many months of searching, emotions, praying, and waiting, I was reading a letter from my biological mother. To think that this instrumental figure, who usually shapes and guides a life, I had known hardly anything personal about before I read her letter. Although the letter still left some gaps of knowledge unfilled, at least I had more answers and the "possibility" for future communications.

Margaret indicated that she had suffered over the years through all of this. This was in response to my questions of if she ever thought of me and how she managed to keep two children, yet give one away? I really did not want to hurt her or sound harsh in asking such questions, but I knew my letter may have been the only chance I had, and my questions were coming from a mother of two, making their inclusion an easy decision at the time. If anything, I thought it would help me understand her decision, if I could gauge from her letter whether or not it had been easy for her, if she still had a connection, wanted me. Through this risk, I learned I had not been forgotten.

I was once again filled with emotions, yet all of them positive now. After finishing the letter, I thanked the Lord for this blessing! I was in a state of disbelief as I reread it again and again. Feelings of elation, a light and airy tingle, coursed through my body with every word I reread and read again. As I took in the words, it was like breathing outside on a cold, crisp winter's day. To think, I found my needle! I did not want to mention this to my mother, as I was not sure how she would take it. As I shared everything with Alonzo, he could not help but be astounded, repeatedly saying, "You found her!" He joked about me being a good detective.

Now, I felt like the ball was in my court again in terms of communication. Although she did not list her phone number in her letter, I did have her correct address. I wanted to give her a little space, so I started to draft another letter that I planned to send out to her in a few weeks time. Although I still had many questions, this letter, this response, began to noticeably fill the hole of worry and doubt I had for the better. I started to have a small, but growing, sense of satisfaction and closure now. Pieces were falling into place. What a blessing in how they fell for me. This particular piece left me emotionally excited, to finally have written confirmation, a communication that validated all of my steps that I had taken in this journey to this point.

I went to church the following Sunday after receiving Margaret's letter and the sermon was centered on Mother's Day. What made it especially pertinent was that the pastor, Reverend James B. Walker, spoke about mothering in all of its forms; spiritual, physical, and adoptive, it all really hit home. He went into great detail about what being a mother really means.

I truly felt then and there, everything that had so suddenly happened to me, was part of God's plan, how I should be grateful and forgiving, especially when it came to some of the feelings of anger I still had toward my adoptive mother. It was all meant to be, in the way my life was continuing to unfold before my eyes.

The sermon made me think of whom I had come to accept for so long as my mother, someone who cared for me and took me in, but I had to wonder, could she ever truly have unconditional love for a child born out of an affair with another woman? Was I a constant reminder of the adultery in her life? Did I remind her of bad feelings? I reflected on times when my mother made comments that seemed arbitrary at the time, but now, they seemed important.

One time I had gotten in trouble for lying about being on

the phone past the time allotted to me. I was talking to my boy-friend at the time, Alonzo. I distinctly recalled her saying, under her breath, "You cannot help it anyway."

Then, I remembered replying, confused, "What?" as she said back flustered, "Nothing."

I wondered now if her comment was due to the fact that I was born out of an adulterous relationship, built on lies and mis-trust that she had still not completely forgiven.

Similarly, I also remembered back to my high school years, when I got a report card with five out of six classes showing A's and B's, but one class I had a warning in it. My mother was re-ally upset and focused only on this one negative grade. I in turn remember being really disappointed with myself.

It also made more sense why I had always been called a daddy's girl. I remember crying in front of him, saying, "She always picks out the negative; can't she ever think anything I do is good enough?"

I was sobbing as I asked this to my father, while she was right there. Later, I remember her coming in my room after they spoke for a few minutes, and she was almost apologetic. This encounter felt strange at the time, because it was not usually what had happened. I had come from a "children should be heard and not seen" upbringing, one where parents were always right. There-fore, this level of acknowledgement was hard to understand back then. I just thought, to myself, "Wow, she heard me," but ironi-cally, this scenario came back to me in a whole new light now. It was almost like he must have said you are being hard on her (my daughter, unspoken).

I continued to pursue this train of thought, thinking to myself, "How would I have raised a child if that situation hap-pened to me, especially considering how strongly I believe in monogamy and fidelity?"

To be born out of something I despise was hard to accept, although I had no control over it. Truthfully, I did not think if that happened to me that I could have raised my husband and his lover's child as my own. She was obviously a better and stronger person than I ever could be in that respect. I knew this clearer understanding would help to soften my previously building angst toward her over the year, which I felt I owed her. All in all, the topic at church that day truly took me on some considerable, introspective reflection.

Then, upon arriving home, I found out that "Secrets & Lies," the movie I had seen only a piece of earlier, would be playing again in its entirety later that day. This only added more sentiment to my already very emotionally powerful day, being able to watch the whole movie through this time.

As if my day could not get any heavier, at approximately 2:30 pm, the telephone rang.

My husband answered as I heard him say, "Yes… yes… here she is," as he excitedly motioned me over to the phone.

I inquired, "Who is it?" in which he whispered a very surprising response, "Margaret".

Still trying to wrestle with what he said, I cautiously said, "Hello," as a springy voice responded, "Hello darling, how are you?"

It took me a minute to comprehend who I was actually talking to; having to reorient myself to the reality I was now living in. Oh my goodness, it was my biological mother! She continued talking, and the experience was honestly somewhat uncomfortable at first, being caught off-guard for something I would have rehearsed much more for had I known she was calling.

Keep in mind it was Mother's Day in the U.S., and I had just watched "Secrets & Lies," a movie about an upper-class Black woman in England who searches and finds her birth mother who is white and has never told her children or anyone that her daughter ever even existed. How the whole family in turn has a hard time accepting her, it all hit too close to home despite how I tried to shake such thoughts. Needless to say, I could not assume any happy endings just yet. The moving sermon by Reverend Walker also had me still evaluating the concept of motherhood as well. Consumed by everything else from the day, I definitely was not expecting this call from Margaret on top.

I asked her how she was doing, and she indicated she was so happy to finally hear my voice. She confirmed that I had two sisters, one older and one younger. She asked how I found out, and I told her about the call to who I believe was her sister-in-law. She was so amazed that I got through to someone based on my own research, especially how the internet played a role.

When we both seemed too speechless to continue, I filled the silence by stating, "Happy Mother's Day!"

She replied "Oh, is it Mother's Day there?"

I responded, "Yes - I thought that is why you picked today to call."

She answered, "No, I had no idea. It is not Mother's Day over here."

Apparently, Mother's Day in England and the United States falls in two different months, something I had no idea of before now. As a result, this was another one of those "ordaincidents" that had been occurring for me since the very beginning. She gave me her phone number and told me she was so pleased to be able to talk.

She concluded with, "Love you," catching me off guard, to then fumble to say back, "Happy Mother's Day Margaret."

I could not find it in myself to call her mom, just yet, so it was a little strange.

Then, I ended the conversation by stating, "Talk to you soon."

Wow, what a Mother's Day - everything leading up to that point. She actually called me; how amazing was that? I was so happy for the remainder of the day. It all felt so surreal. I still had not shared my communications with Margaret with my adoptive mother, the woman I still saw as and called my mom. Realistically, she was the only mother I knew I had for over 30 years. For this reason alone, I felt she was more than enough deserving of such a title.

Margaret and I went on to exchange several more calls and letters over the next few months. I would mainly write just to get to know her better, but there were questions that continued to stay on my mind and occasionally find their way onto the page. During one of our exchanges, I asked her a few important ones, one being to learn more about the story they provided the family services agency about my parents being my aunt and uncle. How did that come about? As it turns out, she explained how my father and she made it up.

I also wanted to know about the relationship between her and her husband. She wrote that he was very controlling and forced her to give me up. She actually said she never got over it emotionally. In the end, their relationship declined and she ended up divorcing him, which I came to learn was a bold move for her both culturally and financially. Divorce is so common now, but a decision for a single mom with two children to make back then was a difficult and uncommon one. Through some of her comments and conversations, I began to identify her as a very strong and independent woman, traits I had always admired and felt I aspired to myself.

I really wanted to see what she looked like, so in one of our exchanges several months later I asked her to send me some photos. When they arrived, I was so excited. There was one picture where she looked very similar to me, not only in some of our features, but even in our poses and stances.

As I looked at the photos in awe, I thought about how I was so closely connected to this individual and never had a clue about it for so many years. I also reminded myself how fortunate I was to be collecting more pieces of the daunting, yet exciting puzzle that had become my past, my life. Throughout these discoveries, I was so thankful for the positive progression our relationship took. I was grateful for her being so receptive of me the entire time.

Before I knew it, over half of a year had passed of us writing letters back and forth and conversations. We had now arrived at a point where we just began to have normal exchanges without all of the sometimes-uncomfortable questions and answers sprinkled in. I was also now beginning to want to have a face-to-face visit. I had previously curbed my enthusiasm with the realization that because we were so many miles apart, it required us to take our relationship slower than if she had lived nearby in the United States.

From the first letter I received to the day I finally made my next step toward knowing Margaret through purchasing my airline tickets, after much thought, it had been a little over one year. I was not sure how my mother would respond to me wanting to go and visit Margaret. Furthermore, I also did not know how my sisters would respond either.

Alonzo and I had thought long and hard about this decision and he ultimately supported me. Although he hated to fly, he was going to take this 10-hour flight with me. While flights were expensive, I wanted to pay for them outright, so I began to save up for a couple of months. I did not want to have a burdensome debt left from such an important trip, especially if it did not go as I prayed it would.

As my life came closer to this next chapter, I knew it was time to tell my mom that I was going to meet Margaret. It felt like the respectable thing to do. I remember going up to her house very nervous, hiding my anxiety, and starting to have a normal conversation about my kids to set the stage for my verbal declaration to come.

Shortly thereafter, I finally revealed, now a year later, "I heard back from Margaret."

She replied in a fairly straightforward manner, "You did?

That is nice."

I went on, "I want to take a trip to visit her in March. I have not been to England in years, and it would be good to go back."

Mom asked, seemingly more interested now, "So, how is she doing?"

"She was fine when I last spoke to her."

She asked intrigued, "Is she still married?"

I clarified, "No, she is divorced".

Appearing to change subjects, she inquired, "Did you say anything to Alicia?"

"No, I have not, isn't that what you asked?"

"I didn't know if they were going with you, which is why I asked".

"No, just Alonzo and I will be going."

Surprisingly, she actually did not seem upset. Apparently I had worked myself up over nothing, overthinking how she might react to me telling her. I got the impression that talking about the past with her was more difficult than moving forward through a relationship with Margaret. With her blessing, I could now fully commit myself to the journey ahead. I left her feeling freer and as if I was continuing on the right path.

-CHAPTER 7-
FLIGHT

I wandered with wonder over what this journey might hold; how would my sisters receive me? My imagination was running away on me again, but I was enjoying every minute in this state of mind. It was also an interesting irony of sorts for me, to think I had family on my mother's side that also lived in England. I needed to spend time with them as well, but how would I explain to them who I had been staying with for the first half of our trip?

I still did not really know who knew and who did not. However, this was my mother's brother and his wife after all. Earlier, I asked my mom if they knew, and she said she did not think so. Once again, she could not remember. My mother's ability to recall memories seemed to be becoming increasingly and frustratingly selective.

In preparation, we packed an array of photos and items, such as: videotapes, special honors the kids had received, newspaper clippings, and whatever else to help fill in the gaps of over 30 years of time, no easy task. Having considered the sheer length of this timespan, it resulted in a lot of packing. However, I wanted to make a good impression, and all of the time that went into my preparation I felt was worth it. I wanted all aspects of me to look good for Margaret. In all actuality, I guess I was just thinking and acting like a daughter who desires to please her mother.

Meanwhile, with all of my focus on getting ready to leave, I realized my hair felt dry and brittle from the winter months. My focus on the past had caused me to overlook my present state. As a result, I needed to do something with my hair, fast. Upon this realization, and without hesitation, I quickly tried to schedule a hair appointment with my hairdresser. I made it with her for the following Thursday.

Unfortunately, on the day of the appointment, my hairdresser wasn't there. Ugh! This news was something I would have normally been slightly upset over, but not made a big deal about. However, for this trip, everything had to be right. My hair was no exception. Instead, my nerves began shouting from the edge of my chair at my mind that was now running from one disappointing hair horror story to the next. I was literally going crazy over such truthfully minor thoughts. If my hairstylist was there my hair would look just the way I like it. Where could I get a walk-in appointment with someone that I felt could help?

So quickly my endeavor to look nice for my family and present myself well was becoming unhinged. There was not enough time to find someone new who I knew I would be happy with. Fortunately, with calming breath, I leveled my head and soon had myself an appointment for early the next morning before our departure flight. With my mind at ease once more, I spent the rest of the day getting everything together for the kids.

My children were very helpful throughout my packing process. Oh how I wished they could go, on one hand, but it was just not possible. In truth, I did not know how Alonzo and I would even be received, much less also bringing our children into a situation that may be emotional and perhaps too overwhelming to just have thrown onto them so suddenly. Plus there was still that cloud I was not allowed to simply blow away, my lingering secret.

I had a hard time gathering myself to say goodbye to my children, especially as my youngest, Ashley, was not used to being away from me. As a result, she had a bit of separation anxiety, to say the least. She was still crying every day when I dropped her off at daycare.

Stress returned in recurring waves when thinking about how Ashley would fare for eight whole days without me. I knew she would be in loving and caring hands, but I knew deep down she just wanted her mom. Although Alicia was more independent and would miss me too, I was sure she would handle it much better. In fact, this process, the preparation to leave, made me think about how my daughters and I were having a mutually-hard time leaving each other. It made me wonder, "If I am having these feelings from just a planned weeklong separation, what does a parent feel inside knowing he/she will separate from his/her child possibly forever?" How difficult it must be living with the resulting unknown that may only be returned to in what-ifs and dreams.

After a restless night, I went for my hair appointment. I left the appointment unsatisfied and felt like I would look terrible for my first impression. However, it was not long before my hair became a distant worry as I fathomed what might happen in the day ahead instead. I felt as though I was already buckled in for an emotional rollercoaster ride with no signs of the excitement ending anytime soon.

Lost in thought, before I knew it, we were at the airport, so excited, armed with cameras, video cameras, addresses, phone numbers, and directions. We were finally on our way there! The flight would actually be taking off momentarily. While Alonzo was mainly nervous because he did not like to fly, I was anxious about everything else for the two of us that lay ahead on this ride that was life, where one cannot always anticipate all of the highs and lows to come.

We got on board at Bradley International Airport in Windsor Locks, Connecticut, headed to our transfer flight in

Ohio. Everything was in motion! Our flight only had a minor 15-minute delay, which was nothing to complain about. Maybe the trip would not be bad at all.

Once on the plane, my husband made sure he was buckled in tight as we both prepared for take-off. I could not believe it was really happening. Before I knew it, the plane was in the air, and there was no turning back. During the flight, I kept visualizing the front of her house, our greeting, everything. I thought about what the meeting would feel like. Would it be awkward or comfortable?

Different emotions cycled through my mind as the flight flew closer and closer. My energy level was as high as the plane was flying that day. As it was early spring, I just optimistically hoped we would not encounter any major weather issues during our trip.

When we arrived at the airport for our transfer to continue our trip to England, we quickly hurried to the next gate. However, as we neared it, I noticed very few people actually waiting there. My legs slackened, becoming heavy and full of dread. As we walked up to the desk, we asked an employee if the flight to England was running late.

She replied, "No, it already left ten minutes ago," which caused my heart to sink.

Speechless, I managed to mutter, "It is already gone...that cannot be." We had followed the plan set by our travel agent as instructed. Specifically, we had been informed the plane would not leave until 2:15 at the earliest.

She responded apologetically, "Sorry, he should have given you more time for an international transfer." My husband and anyone else in close proximity would have seen the crushing disappointment consuming my face.

Alonzo proceeded to read my mind and asked for me, "When will the next plane to England be going out, and can we get on it?"

Unfortunately, she responded, "Maybe tomorrow." She did not believe any more flights were leaving that day.

It was at that point that my eyes began to tear uncontrollably. I could not help it. This trip had been built up so high, as something so important to me. I could not lose any more time, having already missed 30 years. Futilely, I tried to calm myself through deep breathing. Then I started thinking, even worse, she had someone waiting for us at the airport. How would I let him know now? I walked away from the attendant and my husband, as I bowed my head.

I prayed, "Lord, you know how important this trip is for me. This delay could throw the trip off and may also become a financial burden if we have to stay overnight and get additional tickets. Please make something available today."

Just then, Alonzo walked over to me saying, "It is going to be all right," although he looked as if he was as broken-hearted as I was. We walked back to the attendee together, this time with added hope and faith behind us.

I inquired, "Could we go on another flight if you have any?" She checked for us out of courtesy. The amount of typing she went on to perform sounded like she was creating a manuscript, and how time slowed made it feel as long as one, although in all actuality it probably took her under five minutes. Seeing the look on my face, she went on to call another airline. Her expression soon changed as our prayers were answered! She was able to find a flight leaving in just about two hours.

I exclaimed, "Thank you so much!"

As this was such a vital trip for me, I was immensely relieved. My husband and I hugged and then proceeded to the other airline to make the necessary changes and get something to eat. Remembering my phonebook, I called Margaret and let her know that we would be arriving two hours behind schedule. I also called our kids and my mom to update them.

In less than two hours, we were in line boarding for our

next flight. Whether we wanted to or not, on that flight, we slept, already emotionally drained and knowing we had ten hours left to go. It would be morning by the time we got there. Not to mention, as my body does not easily adjust to time-zone changes, I knew the respite would come in handy.

As the plane flew closer to Europe, we woke up for dinner and discussed our plans. We knew secrets would continue, it seemed inevitable, even after meeting Margaret, since my aunt and uncle also wanted us to visit and stay with them. They would want to know who else we were seeing and staying with. At least at that point, we planned to go to Margaret's house for the first few days, spend a few days with my aunt and uncle, and then the final days with Margaret.

We got our maps, tickets, and money in order for landing. Once we touched ground, we knew we were supposed to have someone meet us there, but we were afraid he may have left due to the delay we had experienced. Although we had contacted Margaret, we were unsure if she was ever able to reach him.

Alonzo asked, "Is this her boyfriend that is picking us up?"

I replied, "I do not know; she made it seem like a family friend."

Once we had everything in order, in faith, we began looking for Mr. Smith. If he was still here, I hoped he would have a sign or something to distinguish him by. We searched for roughly 30 minutes before asking to have him paged. Before long, we began to wonder if we should just find out how far away we were from Margaret's house and get a taxi or train, whatever made the most sense in terms of price and convenience.

Several minutes later, without anyone showing up, we went and began to ask what the best form of transportation was to Margaret's house from Gatwick Airport. Unfortunately, no matter the option, it seemed as if our destination was a good distance away and would be quite costly regardless of the method we chose. With this additional awareness, I needed my prayers to be answered once more. We had come too far for travel issues and added expenses to happen to us now. It was at that moment I closed my eyes and prayed for another answer.

-CHAPTER 8-
ARRIVAL

Right in the middle of the moment of crisis on how we would reach Margaret, my prayers were once again answered. Mr. Smith seemingly appeared out of nowhere.

A tall, middle-aged man, with an athletic build and a perky British accent that had island flair, asked, "Are you Lorna? I have been looking for you for quite a while. Margaret sent me to pick you and your husband up, so let me take your things."

I was very happy that he had stayed and waited, especially seeing as though we were not his guests and he was doing this for Margaret as a favor.

I thought to myself, "He must be a very dedicated friend!"

We then got in his car, which seemed so small compared to our American SUVs and Minivans. My nervousness was slowly turning into confident excitement as I thought about the meeting that would be taking place in under an hour from now. Dreams were becoming an exhilarating reality as we began our drive. My thoughts remained positive during the start of our ride. We had come too far for things to fall apart now.

As we closed in on our destination, Mr. Smith began to tell us all about London. He spoke about the major tourist attractions as we passed them on the way to Lambeth County. As we passed Buckingham Palace, he indicated that you can tell that the

Queen is in by the foot guard and the position of the flag. I also loved the clock Big Ben since I was little, so seeing it with my grown eyes just warmed my heart. I even commented how Ashley would call the tower clock on North Main Street, near downtown Hartford, Big Ben. He also mentioned how nice it was to have a great public transportation system that can take you anywhere you want to go.

After pointing out some landmarks, he inquired, "Have you visited here before?"

To which I replied, "Yes, actually, I was born here."

He responded, "I know when Margaret asked me to pick up her niece from America, I did not know you had lived here prior."

Aware of the part I had been unknowingly cast to play, I responded, "Yes."

Although unable to dull my day, I was reminded again of my cloud, which apparently had flown over here with me. I was still a secret, at least as far as Mr. Smith was concerned, so I could not slip now. Revealing anything to the wrong person had the potential to get my mother, Margaret, or both, upset with me.

I restrained any emotions that may have caused me to act out of character. Feeling light emanating from within me, I knew that no matter what I had to do or could not say, this was going to be a good visit. I was finally meeting Margaret after all! Regardless of who did or did not know, at least she and I would always know the truth.

Before I knew it, he tells us we are almost there. In that moment, the beauty of the surroundings hit me and my cloud excuses itself to let me soak in the present in all its immediacy. The warm sun is really shining down and I notice how beautiful a day it will be. There is not a drop of dreary weather, fog or rain; today, it is wonderful.

Mr. Smith actually says, "You must have brought the sunshine with you, as it has not been this sunny in a while."

As he navigates the final streets nearing Margaret's house, I have this strange feeling in my stomach and the rest of my body, as if I had been here before. My inner light begins to grow. It all feels so very familiar. It is truly a God moment. There is no other way to explain it. My husband and I have been holding hands during the entire ride and I start to squeeze his more and more in anticipation. One of my biggest support systems, he is always happy when I am happy. No surprise then, he is absolutely elated.

Mr. Smith lets us know our destination is just up the street.

"Just around the bend," as he puts it.

We are almost there! I am watching each street name go by. Soon, I notice the street sign for the address I had for my sister that Faith had provided to me. I then see Ballimory Road. We are almost at the address that I have spent so much time searching for, the pot-of-gold address at the end of my rainbow of a search, the physical needle in the haystack. When I see her address, there is Margaret, standing in front of her door, smiling, in person. Her front yard is filled with beautiful flowers, but I cannot take my eyes off of her. It feels like I am about to be born all over again. The glowing inside of me is impossible to hide. I am meeting my mummy!

My husband whispers in excitement, "There she is!"

I calmly, well, as calmly as I can, get out of the car and say, "Hello."

I go to grab my purse and my suitcase, but Alonzo steps in, "I have it."

Therefore, I just leave my things and start walking toward the house. I stop to thank Mr. Smith for bringing us and waiting, even with our delay.

He replies, "No problem, dear."

Margaret and I are walking toward one another. I feel like a little girl and a giant at the same time. Our hug, a releasing embrace that bares so much energy and anticipation, is a true adult rebirth, where it feels as if your mother is holding you for the first time. She grins and makes what I think is a little nervous laughter herself. Any passersby would swear we were both glowing, filling the air with tremendous warmth and feeling.

She says, "Hello my darling."

I experience a sudden, yet subtle, feeling of tranquility as I look at her. It seems as if the sun is shining from inside of me as I look at this cheerful woman. My feelings of joy, excitement, and awkwardness are all balled up in the elated pit of my stomach that had housed the light we just shared with the world. I think to myself, wow, she looks good, especially for someone 21 years my senior! I automatically want to search for any similarities. I look her over and soon notice we are both the same height and body shape. She is actually the same size, which seems so strange. Up until now, I have been used to mothers generally being heavier than their daughters.

The past returns and mixes with the present as we all then walk inside. Her house was quaint and lovely, nicely decorated, yet comfortable. It was traditional, yet modern, at the same time. I was now a voyeur looking at the surroundings, as if I was not supposed to be there. I soaked in every detail. I had to soak it all in as much as possible, as I did not know if I would ever see it again. To own her own home as a single woman, she must have been pretty savvy. She had grown up in an era where the husband was seen as the provider. However, as I already knew, Margaret was not just any woman.

She showed us to our room, where we put our things. Although Alonzo and I were still very tired at the time, seeing her, actually being there, gave us each the boost of energy we needed. It was about 1:30 p.m. there, and she was already cooking brunch.

She then invited us to the table, "Come and have something to eat."

Now, I am a picky eater, so I was secretly thinking, I hope it is something I like. I would not want to seem rude accidentally at our first meal or be caught pretending to enjoy something I did not. To my surprise, she made one of my favorite foods, fried plantains. Was that a coincidence? She also introduced me to my cousin, Vanessa, who lived with her. She would be our liaison to the rest of the family, making her even more important to get to know a great deal more about.

Her presence was especially helpful, as I hoped to largely limit the exploring of history with Margaret to the exchanging of photos and other artifacts. I really did not want to drill her for information in her home with even more questions, especially because many of them had already been answered, at least in part, since the original letters were sent about year and a half ago. I wanted to start our visit fresh and enjoy the time itself for what it was. The visuals at that moment, being in her home, the weight of just being there, seeing her in the flesh, spoke to me much more than words or answers ever could. Sometimes it is best to just live in the moment.

As we learned after our delicious meal, Vanessa was in her 20s and had just had a baby three weeks before our arrival. The circumstances surrounding our meeting were good for the both of us, as I could share some loving guidance on parenting myself, since this was her first child, a beautiful baby girl. In turn, I could benefit from someone who was home all day to fill me in on any family history I did not already know while Margaret was working or busy.

I asked her, "Did you know I was coming and who I am?"

She told me, "Yes," then proceeded to share a story.

As it turned out, Margaret had shown her a letter. It had come up because one day she saw Margaret sitting on the front steps, curiously, after receiving her mail. She seemed pale and dazed. Vanessa asked her if anything was wrong, so Margaret just handed her the letter and asked that she read it. It was the letter that I had written to her, indicating that I was her daughter and wanted to find her. Vanessa indicated that Margaret seemed almost relieved when she handed her the letter. I can imagine what a burden it would have been to hold a secret like that in for so many years.

I wondered if although Margaret had shared this secret with her, who she treated like a daughter, had she told my sisters? I hoped an answer would arise without any prompting. In response to me asking in general about my sisters, it turned out Vanessa had already called my younger sister Linda, who would be over later the next day. She indicated that Linda had heard a brief mention of me, but she did not know I was actually here visiting now.

That evening, as Margaret cooked dinner, we talked about other family members I did not know I had in the U.S., particularly in Boston, Massachusetts; New York, New York; and Florida. Margaret admitted most of them did not know about me. It made me think about how a pregnancy would be easier to hide from family that was not living nearby.

However, there was one of her brothers who had made a comment to her one time when she went to Jamaica with her two girls to visit. She reflected on him saying, "I thought you had three girls?" She said she never really responded to his question.

We went on to eat another great meal. She was a really good cook. Flavorful chicken, rice and peas, and steamed vegetables. My husband could not believe the mounting similarities between the two of us, saying Margaret and I had very similar mannerisms, personalities, hair, skin texture, and more. Alonzo and I kept catching each other gazing at one another in wonder and amazement time and time again.

After dinner, Vanessa, my husband, and I, went for a walk to see the wonderful neighborhood. As we walked, we went down a couple of streets and actually had to go past the street where my older sister lived. Of all the coincidences, as we were approaching, she happened to be bringing out the trash. It seemed as though I might be meeting Sharon sooner than I had anticipated.

I only knew it was her because Vanessa said, "It looks like Sharon is putting out trash, that is actually her right over there."

I asked, "Maybe you can introduce us?"

Vanessa then went up and spoke to her briefly, before referencing us by saying, "This is Lorna and her husband from America."

It felt as if my heart had frozen in unease once this introduction escaped her lips, praying in that moment for a warm reception before it beat again.

Sharon just kind of looked at us, seemingly indifferent, said "Hi," then returned to her conversation with Vanessa as if I had already started walking away.

Alonzo and I soon did just that and continued walking past, as I did not want to feel as if I was pushing myself on her. My heart willed itself to beat again, although unsatisfied.

My husband put his arm around me and said "I am sorry. I know that was not what you expected, but give it time, it may change."

However, try as I might, I could not help but feel awful and concluded that she must be angry about the whole situation for some reason and maybe even toward me, as a result. It was unfortunate to end the day on this unexpected, yet actual, note.

I thought to myself, "It is not like I put myself up for adoption and advocated for this whole secret."

Well, at least I got to see what she looked like face-to-face if nothing more were to come of us interacting during the rest of our time there. She was a very attractive woman, with an oddly familiar face. Was it because I had dreamed of her or something more? I tried to not let her weigh on my mind, as my mind had been in such a heightened state until now.

I rationalized that I did not go into encountering her with either a positive or negative expectation. There had not been much time to think at all when placed on the spot so suddenly. Of course, a positive response would have been preferable. What made it so difficult was that it felt like no reaction whatsoever, which I internalized as a negative one.

Vanessa soon caught up with us, and I commented, "I thought you said she is generally easygoing with things? Her facial expression seemed like, 'why are you talking to me?'"

She replied, "No, it was that she was completely caught off guard. I will talk to her again tomorrow."

I hoped that Vanessa was speaking the truth and felt a little better, making me look forward to having another chance to connect with Sharon while we were there. During our walk, we also came across a local market and bus station, which would soon come in handy, as we planned to venture out the next day.

We then went back for the night to rest. Margaret asked us if we needed anything before she went to bed, and we stated things were fine. Overall, the day was great. Before I fell asleep, I prayed in my heart that it was just a misunderstanding with Sharon. I wanted to experience what it was like to have sisters who treated me like family.

-CHAPTER 9-
SISTERHOOD

The next morning was a new day, one of which Alonzo and I spent in large part visiting various museums and shops by train. We were there for a reunion, but we were still thousands of miles away from home. Therefore, we wanted to make a vacation of it. I was amazed at how clean and easy to use the subway was.

The saying "mind the gap," posted all over the rail system, read like a sign for much more than just watching your step. Spiritually, we talk about standing in the gap for someone. Every time I saw the sign, I thought of my mom standing in the gap for Margaret and how the Lord allowed this gap of unknown knowledge to slowly be filled.

Several wonderful sights later, we returned to Margaret's house. Vanessa told me that Linda would be coming over shortly.

I thought to myself, "Okay, I am going to meet my other sister properly and pray it works out better than the last encounter with Sharon did."

Vanessa and I went on to talk more about that encounter from last night and she reassured me how both of my sisters are very nice. I played with her baby all the while we spoke. Although I had offered to cook earlier, Margaret and Vanessa once again already had things taken care of.

I responded, "I will make breakfast tomorrow then, as I love to cook."

When Linda finally arrived, I still did not know what to expect. She came off much more receptive as Vanessa introduced us. It even worked out better that Margaret was not there when she arrived, because I think, at least for myself, it felt a little freer to speak without any worry of possibly offending anyone with any conversations around questions that might come up.

Although Linda initially attended to and gave most of her attention to the baby, showing me a warming interest, she soon started talking to me. Having been raised alone, as an only child, here I was looking at this gorgeous, fit young woman, who was also so much more than that. She was also my little sister. Inside, I was swelling with a strange sense of pride, of which I had no real reason to even take credit for. She appeared very proper, and in a short period of time, I witnessed her quick wit too. I was already feeling blessed to have her for a sister, even though we had just met.

She wondered, "How did you come to know about mummy?"

In response, I gave her the entire story, stating how I had only known for two years myself.

She replied, "Well, that is better than me, because I barely heard more than a mum. One day, when mummy was gardening, I stopped to talk to her. We were having a routine conversation, and out of nowhere, she says, 'by the way, you have another sister,' without divulging any further details or explanations. She also had not told us you were coming to visit."

There was now no question that there was still some tension and secrets around me, but I could tell it was not directed toward me. As I asked more questions about her and Sharon, I began to ponder how my birth and leaving had impacted Margaret and her relationship with her children. As we talked, it seemed like I had left lasting changes on this family.

Not to be judgmental, but it seemed like my departure had especially affected Margaret's relationship with Linda, who had been born just ten months after me. It was funny listening to Linda talk about herself and her sister. She sounded like a therapist, very intuitive in nature.

As we were talking, at one point it was almost as if she had an ah-ha moment, where she said, "I often felt I was not good enough, or I was not special enough. It all makes sense now."

Such statements and accompanying expressions made me realize just how deep gaps can be. Here was a biological daughter, who clearly loved her mom, expressing their relationship struggles throughout the years. I thought it sounded similar to my mom and me.

I asked if she thought Margaret and I shared any similar physical traits, and while she noticed some, she was also quick to point out that you cannot attribute everything to heredity, because you could meet anyone on the street who happens to have the same traits or characteristics as you. I guess I was just looking for some more "connectors."

I soon noted, "I was surprised that neither of you had children," instantly regretting how I phrased this remark.

This statement was only because, in my mind, I figured we were all around the same age and the likelihood of both sisters having no children was slim, statistically speaking. It was hard to believe that I currently had Margaret's only two grandchildren, and if I had not ever found out about my adoption, she may have never had the experience of being a grandmother.

Linda replied, "Well, mothering and daughtering is an experience, but I guess we just have not gone that route yet."

Trying to correct myself, I clarified, "Oh no, I definitely understand. I just thought how she now has two grandchildren and before that seemed to have none."

We continued to talk. She really gave me a glimpse into Margaret as a person, who appeared to be a very private person.

Linda talked about how Margaret kept everything close to the breast. She was a strong and stern parent, who had high expectations for her children.

She also told me more about how Margaret had been divorced for a while and how she really held it together well afterward. I went on to ask about her father, Margaret's husband, and it seemed as if their relationship had been strained, but she was beginning to explore reconnecting with him. He, it turns out, was a very strict disciplinarian.

Throughout these revelations, the filling of gaps, I could not help but be fascinated. I felt like I was on the other side of the room, watching the two of us have this very personal and intense conversation. She was so upfront and direct, in a refreshing sort of way. I had to also keep reminding myself that she really just found out herself. If I was still trying to comprehend everything, she really must have been thinking things through still.

It was easy to idealize what my life would have been like if I had lived with them. I had especially thought, at least before having this conversation, how I may have been happier with my sisters and Margaret. This was especially true when I heard more about dance class and lessons and some of things I had never had the chance to do. However, the more I listened to the stories of their father's passion for corporal punishment, and thinking about how he would have felt toward me, it poked a small hole in my fairytale balloon of how happy I could have been.

We continued to talk and I told her more about what I knew about the relationship between my father and her mother. They met in a house or flat my mother and father owned. They had a brief affair and Margaret became pregnant. One of Linda's big questions was how Margaret knew I was his if she was married at the time. One of the things I told her was how Margaret had said that she was separated at the time of the relationship.

I clarified that I only came to know about most of these facts through conversations with my mother. She had shared these things somewhat reluctantly, and I had also found some answers out through the search process, which provided me with documents and materials to help me piece information together. I had also gathered some information from Margaret through our correspondences. Basically, the knowledge I had was a patchwork of information in my attempt to continue to make the most sense of my new reality.

During our conversation, I felt like I got some real facts out of it, not just small talk. Linda provided me with a much closer look into my biological mother, mummy: her style, her strength, her demeanor, and her suppression of the pain that my sisters did not know existed for most of their lives. Her description of their life provided me with insight that helped to bring greater context to everything I had already known.

Amid our talk, there was one topic in particular that I found especially fascinating. About two years prior to this trip to London, my husband and I took a weekend excursion. We had both been working so hard and had been so busy that we just wanted to take a simple vacation. As a result, he had us go for a weekend getaway to a local waterfront pier. There, they had seafood restaurants, with kiosk boutiques, and an outdoor mall. We just walked around and visited the booths and stores, enjoying one another's company. One of our stops happened to be a woman on the pier that had a sign stating, "Read your palm. For fun."

My husband said, "Go ahead and do it."

I replied, "I really do not believe in that stuff."

The woman then interjected, "It is just for fun."

I told her, "Only God knows my future," to which she responded, "Mam, Jesus is the head of my life and all that I do comes from him."

Finally giving in, I decided, "Well then, I don't mind."

I just did not want to deal with any negative forces. Compared to where I was with my faith at the time of visiting Margaret, I would not have even done it just for fun now because of my growing beliefs and biblical understanding.

I sat down as she took my hand and began to look at and hold it.

She noted, "There are some interesting things I get from you, one is someone soon in your family is going to come into some money and it will be helpful to you."

The second thing she said was with a very strange look on her face, "There has been a big secret, a cloud over your entire life; the cloud is going to be lifted within the next year."

I remember telling her, "Everything in my life is fine," in response.

There was no cloud or secret known to me then. Her comments instead seemed so far off base, yet she remained adamant. We just laughed it off, having enjoyed ourselves, and thanked her for her time. It was this memory that came back to me when I was speaking with Linda. While the cloud that came never fully left, apparently there had been one after all.

Surprisingly, during the same timeframe, Linda was at a local fair in London and had stopped at a fortune teller who told her that she had two sisters, which she corrected by explaining how she only had one. The fortune teller disagreed and reiterated that there were three. She too thought it was odd, going so far as to later share this encounter with Sharon.

Wow! We thought that was so amazing. Not for the nature of the discovery, but that we shared similar experiences about unknown secrets. We just looked at each other like it was all too much, our bodies trying to process everything that had transpired up until this point in our lives. Emotionally overwhelmed, we ended there and embraced. I told her it was great to meet her, and she shared with me the same. We hoped to see each other again before I left.

After she departed, Vanessa said, "I am glad you had a chance to meet her."

"It was nice to see her, and I am glad we had a chance to

learn more about each other."

That evening, once Margaret returned from work, I told her how I had the chance to meet Linda. She seemed so happy that this encounter had occurred and that it also went so well. Although I did not say anything else about it, I wondered why she did not tell my sisters that I was coming. Perhaps she was leaving some things up to fate too? I concluded that it must have been too hard for her to bring it up with them without opening the doors to many other questions as a result. Are some things better left unsaid?

The next morning, Sharon called Vanessa and wanted for us to come over that evening. I was very excited by her initiative, seeing how our last encounter did not seem as if she wanted to make any further communication whatsoever. In my preparation of meeting her again, I reflected on the movie on television the first time Margaret called, "Secrets & Lies," starring Marianne Jean-Baptiste, and how one of the issues in it was the challenge for siblings to get along with a sister they previously had never known existed. I tried to push my doubts away and not let them cloud the memories I had made.

Fortunately, that evening, we walked over to see Sharon and she was, happily, completely different from last time she received Alonzo, Vanessa, and me. She welcomed us with a beautiful smile and hug. My body let out a sigh of relief in this embrace, and I concluded that I had made the wrong impression the day before.

As Vanessa had suggested, Sharon explained to me that she was not mad or ever trying to ignore me, she was just caught off-guard. She had not known I was here or even much about me in general. Likewise, as it turned out, she had heard the same nonchalant "you have a sister" mention from Margaret. At the time, she did not know what to say, feeling it best not to say anything at all.

In my observations of Sharon, she was a very cheerful

woman, ageless it seemed. She looked at least six years younger than how old she actually was. The fact that she was older than me was hard to believe. She also had a very light and fun personality. She was around my height, with dark wavy hair, and was absolutely beautiful.

I told her how she had a nice home, very modern, reminiscent of homes I knew back in the United States, filled with all types of gadgets and electronics. Throughout our time together, she genuinely seemed interested in our lives. I showed her many of the photos Alonzo and I had brought with us.

Her enjoyment of music also became increasingly apparent. Sharing a similar passion, as a result, we took many opportunities to connect over the artists we liked, with her actually knowing more than I did about various musical groups and the lyrics to their songs. I was mostly amazed by just being able to have a conversation with my sister like sisters would have.

I also met her fiancé, Larry, who arrived partway through our visit. He was a tall, athletic-looking man, with very distinct features. They made for a really nice looking couple. As it turned out, it was actually his father who was the one who had picked us up from the airport. He had the same look of uncertainty that we all shared, at least momentarily, upon first meeting.

I also took the opportunity to ask her a different set of questions since she was older than me. I often wondered, even though she would have been very young, if she had any memories of me?

She said, "I have often had these vague, faint memories of a baby, but probably because our sister was born eleven months after you. It may have all just blurred together."

She continued, "I remember a baby coming up the stairs."

This memory made me wonder about her age again – Margaret had said Sharon was only two years old at the time, yet she apparently remembered me.

I told her, "It is so weird. I often remember a reddish tabby cat, yet we did not ever have one."

She replied intrigued, "Well, we had a red-orange tabby cat."

Now I know research has revealed memory development starts much later in life, but this cat was still something so vivid in my memory. Interestingly, I also always had a strange, but comforting, sensation when I drank juice or beverages from squirt-like bottles. I would tell my husband that it was as if there was a connection to the soothing feeling I got from them. I wondered if I unknowingly had such a hard time with my separation from Margaret that a bottle was my sense of security through it all. If I was still drinking from a bottle when I went to live with who I would go on to call my parents, it made me wonder if the separation created some trauma, and I found comfort through a baby bottle.

Even though I had been away for just a few days, I already could not stop thinking about how hard it must be for my six year-old back home, never mind imagining how she would have reacted if she never saw me again. She actually had to speak to me each night during our vacation trip, which I was more than happy to oblige. Talking with Sharon made me momentarily scrutinize these things and then return to just talking, growing closer.

She was also very interested in my regional television program, which I did in addition to my full time career, and was a fan of many of the artists I had interviewed for it; such as Queen Latifah, Run–D.M.C., LL Cool J, P. Diddy, Sisters with Voices (SWV), The Roots, Alfonso Riberio, Faith Evans, MC Lyte, Ruby Dee & Ossie Davis, and many others. We also talked about home repair and renovation, as she was remodeling her home, and I loved to decorate.

After a great deal of warm conversation, our visit ended just as cordially as it had begun. We shared numbers and agreed to stay in touch. Overall, our time together was much friendlier than I had expected it to be.

-CHAPTER 10-
GROWING CLOSER

Back at Margaret's house, it was obvious that there were a lot of emotions and feelings that still weighed on her mind. As we talked more, I began to turn the conversation back onto her to learn more about her as a person, from her own point of view. She was very knowledgeable about many current events and had strong opinions on the way things should be. Also, she definitely had a strong faith and was clear about what she believed was right and wrong.

I also asked about her work, as she seemed to have several skill sets. I knew she had assisted elderly clients with homecare services. She had actually gone back to school later in life to earn a certificate, as well as studied hairstyling. It was interesting to see just how independent and business-savvy she was.

On the topic of hairstyling, she actually offered, "As a matter of fact, do you want me to do your hair?"

Although I was not thrilled with my hair as it was, I was also not sure how it would turn out. However, as she was pretty adamant, I agreed. I was impressed that she even had a shampoo sink in her own house. It was amazing. I felt like I was at a salon. She had a cape and the various shampoos and everything else to make the experience feel salon-like.

As I would soon realize, her washing my hair was much more than just a shampoo. It was a connection point that I could feel as soon as I sat back to have her wash it. There is a level of intimacy that is shared with anyone that does your hair. You do not let just anyone do it. Therefore, having a mother do a daughter's hair, a daughter who has just reconnected with her, having missed so many years of caring touch from her, was powerful. The situation allowed me to relax, as my body gave in to my birth mother's touch. I was not in a guarded position physically or emotionally the entire time. What a positive reunion story this had become.

As she shampooed and we talked, I thought that this is what mothers and daughters who are close must do. I had spent so much time doing my girls' hair that it had become part of our shared experience. She asked me what products I use and talked about how soft and curly my hair was when I was a baby.

I just absorbed all of the physical and emotional love as the water poured over my head. It was as if each touch was a chance to make amends for the time that had been lost. If I had known I would eventually end up here after receiving the life-altering news of my adoption, I may have handled the initial shock a bit easier then.

This experience was a chance to start over; my heart and hair both benefitted from it. At this time of the year, my hair was somewhat damaged, as I had been dealing with dry hair and skin all winter. I had tried so many things, but nothing seemed to moisturize it.

She continued to gently shampoo and then condition my hair. Next, she dried and set it on rollers. I sat under the dryer for a while, just taking in this time of true reconnection, and then she finally combed me out.

In the end, my hair was so incredibly soft I could not believe it. I had my husband touch my hair and he agreed it was very light and soft. The process of my hair going from dry to feeling softer than it had in years mirrored my internal softening, receiving an unspoken release.

Alonzo also saw this opportunity as very special for her and me to have that time and shared experience together. We all then went out to dinner to celebrate our reunion, as Alonzo and I would be going to spend time with my mother's brother and his wife, but departing with unforgettable memories such as this intact.

My uncle actually came and picked us up from Margaret's home. However, she was not there when he came. Once we got to their house, we were talking about my mom and their childhood.

My uncle then, out of the blue, said, "You were such a pretty little girl when you were young."

In that comment, I wondered if he was alluding to knowing about my adoption or if he was just making a remark. There were also a lot of questions about the "friends" who we were staying with. We surprisingly did a good job covering ourselves.

Alonzo and I then spent the next couple of days with my aunt and uncle in the countryside of London. We went sightseeing and had a totally different, but great time. We visited several more tourist attractions with them and picked up souvenirs for my friends and family. My uncle brought us by several relatives' homes, some whom I had not seen since I was six years old. With each greeting, I wondered who knew. If anyone did, there was no mention.

Although I enjoyed my time with them, I really wanted to get back to see Margaret, because I was trying to catch up on over 32 years of life. Before I knew it, my aunt and uncle were doing just that, bringing me back to her house. Both my aunt and uncle actually came inside with me.

I introduced everyone, and my aunt kept stating that she knew Sharon from somewhere and how she looked so familiar. While some men often just go with things, I do believe most women are more curious or pay more attention to details.

Once again, I pondered, "Did she know who this was?"

I did not even know if they were aware of the whole adoption situation. Additionally, I did not want to create an issue for my mom back in the United States, so I just left things as if these were our friends and nothing more. Even though that meant distorting the truth, something I did not like to do.

Once my aunt and uncle left, we all let out a sigh of relief. We were then scheduled to go to dinner with Linda. Once we got to the restaurant, Alonzo and I noticed how much smaller the portion sizes were, as well as the absence of pork on the menu. In its place was lamb. I also watched how healthy and mindful Linda ate.

Although impressed, I thought, "It must not be a weight-related issue, since she is not overweight."

She explained that is was about overall health, not just weight or size. I saw it as her having a lifestyle of living holistically fit, emotionally, physically, and spiritually. This was her being free.

I ordered my warm blackberry crumble with a side of Bird's Custard. It was a taste that felt incredibly pleasant and familiar with every spoonful. I was so happy with the conversations that I had during the dinner with Linda as well. She was very wise and instinctive for a younger sister. I did wish we lived closer, but was grateful that I even had this chance to be with her.

Shortly thereafter, we were back at the house getting ready for bed and I could not believe it was almost time to go home. However, I could not deny that our reunion went exceptionally well, having in the end exceeded my wildest expectations. Even if I were to never visit again, I at least felt I had the opportunity to meet everyone.

I definitely wanted to continue to cultivate these relationships, but I also knew we were roughly 3,500 miles apart. Furthermore, I also knew that sisterly relationships need work, even if you live near each other. In the end, I walked away with a sense that my adoption had impacted this family, my family, even without my sisters having knowledge of my existence.

Next thing I knew, Alonzo and I were hugging Margaret goodbye. She cried as we were about to leave. I hugged Vanessa, kissed the baby, and hugged Linda. As Sharon had to work, we had exchanged our goodbyes earlier. We were planning to get a ride back with the same individual who had delivered us there, Mr. Smith.

Right before he arrived, Margaret exclaimed, "I am so happy, I do not care who knows! I have three daughters and that is how it is."

I felt as though that statement alone brought her another sense of relief and freedom.

It did something for me in that moment too, but understanding just what it did was cut short with Mr. Smith arriving and her saying to him, "My niece and her husband have an 11 o'clock flight, and I do not want them to be late."

I tried my best to hide an awkward smile that came upon my face as my feeling of newfound freedom seemed to already be sliding backward. Margaret's declaration made me realize there would always be that cloud over me in some form for the foreseeable future. It was just a matter of how I chose to cope with it. Actions and habits are hard to break. Although she may have thought she was ready for everyone to know, she was not entirely yet. However, she accepted me, and I accepted her as who we really were.

Alonzo placed our luggage into the trunk of the car and Mr. Smith stated how we better get going before we miss the flight. While I did not want to miss another flight, I could not help but fondly look around the house one last time, touching the bed, the furniture, and taking in everything, as I did not know if I would ever be back there again. Every part of me thanked the time it had spent there and the many memories made.

We then all hugged again and I thanked everyone. I took a video of the beautiful flowers in the garden and smelled them one more time. We had one last embrace and Margaret said, "love you," as she told us to travel safely. Alonzo opened the door for me, and I slowly entered the car. What a major, life-affirming time I had. All of the time I had invested into getting to this point, meeting Margaret, Vanessa, and my sisters, made it all more than worth it.

Alonzo and I soon got on the plane with our lives permanently changed for the better. I had this whole new family that I could begin to build stronger relationships with. It was my hope my children could also meet them at some point in their lives before anyone passed away. On the flight back, I decided that both my children needed to at least one day know Margaret for who she really was, while she was still alive, once Alonzo and I felt they were ready.

-CHAPTER 11-
NEW RELATIONSHIPS

When I returned home, I spent some time just reflecting, while also being thankful that my life could finally slow down. My journey through this process was one that had taken me through many mixed emotions and a path to healing. I was conscious that my pace, my years of discovery, from finding out, searching for, and finally meeting Margaret, had been tempered. This was due to my ability to lean on my faith in God and the undying and unconditional support from my loving husband. The cycle of my seeking phase brought me a lot of excitement and thrill that had now shifted into a coasting level. I also accepted that Margaret and my sisters being across the world would make it much harder for us to meet as often as if we all lived nearby.

Instead, our correspondences became that of a loving family warmly communicating with one another, who may have lived apart, but now had found each other. I could finally obtain a level of contentment in my new normalcy, which was a breath of fresh air. While my cloud of secrecy was still there, Margaret and my sisters ultimately welcomed me as a daughter and a sister and wanted to continue our relationship. I could not have asked for anything more.

During the several years that followed, I communicated with Margaret and my sisters by letters and then by email. I marveled at how far the internet and computers had come since

I used them for my initial research to find Margaret. Margaret, my sisters, and I first exchanged birthday cards, then presents for Christmas. I learned a lot from our correspondences, especially about Linda, as she would write and journal a lot, making it especially easy for me to find Christmas presents for her.

One big event that brought all of us even closer was when Sharon became pregnant. This was a life event that really seemed to bring my sisters and me to the next level. I got a sense of this through the communications I received from them.

Soon, I had a new niece named Karen, born to my older sister! Learning this news, I was so excited, yet I could not tell anyone. I sent gifts and the book I give everyone that has a baby, "What to Expect the First Year." Although Sharon had not been a big letter writer, her having the baby brought about another reason to connect. She sent pictures of her family, and our communications picked up more regularly after the birth.

Margaret would also send money for our children for Christmas. As a pound is worth more than a dollar, one Christmas I purchased a PlayStation 2 for them with it. I really did not get into the whole videogame-console phase, but I wanted them to get something they would really appreciate that particular year from her.

My daughter Alicia responded, "Wow, Aunt Margaret is really nice! Is she rich?"

I replied, "No she is not."

In her mind, she was thinking how odd it was for this distant aunt to give them such a nice gift. In my mind, I was thinking this is the type of gift a grandparent would give.

During several of our communications, Sharon mentioned how Larry had planned a visit to the United States to visit friends in Florida. I wrote back and told her that she had to visit. We could spend a weekend together, and I would be willing to pay for her ticket if it would help her make it over to the Northeast. She planned to talk about it with her fiance and let me know.

After a couple of months of convincing, they decided to stay with us for a weekend. I was so excited! They would be on our turf! It was also a chance for her to meet my youngest daughter Ashley. I would finally have a chance to meet my one-year-old niece as well.

In preparation, I told my mother that Sharon would be coming to stay with us for a weekend. By this time, my mother had moved in with us and would be sharing the visit with us as a result. She was actually pretty excited herself.

She asked, "Is Margaret also coming?"

I told her, "No she is not. Just Sharon, her family, and a friend are."

As I planned for their arrival, I imagined all of the memories to come that we would make. With my mind lost in eagerness, before I knew it, Alonzo and I were on our way to pick them up. I was so pleased to see them again.

Sharon had cut her hair short since our last visit four years ago. It was amazing how fast time had flown. I knew Larry probably wondered if he would have a good time, as he did not really know us. Karen was a beautiful baby, as everyone that saw her during the trip agreed, exclaiming how she should be in commercials.

I brought them to our house and set them up in Alicia's room, since she was away at Rutgers in New Jersey. Her room had since become our guest room. I fondly watched Sharon, as she was so patient and caring with Karen. Additionally, she was so particular about what her baby ate and only allowed milk and water, no juice for her as a liquid.

She said, "So many people say, why do you not give Karen juice? However, it really is just sugar."

Statements from her such as this made me feel proud to have strong sisters with character. You have to have a strong sense of yourself to do something different than what the majority of society is telling you to do. It did not matter to her that most mothers provide their babies with juice, as she was determined that water and milk was her choice of beverage for her toddler. More than anything, it was refreshing to see her hold her ground around what she thought was the best parenting for her child.

During their stay, we had also been invited to a family cookout on my husband's side of the family. It was a beautiful day, so we decided we should all go together to enjoy the weather and company. We all got packed up and went over to my husband's stepbrother's home. His father, stepmother, a few other relatives, and siblings were there. The setting was just beautiful, as their house is on the scenic Farmington River. The temperature was about 74 degrees outside, with low humidity, and there was so much great barbeque food to eat on top of it all.

At one point, Sharon and I went upstairs into a guest room to change Karen's diaper, and we just started out of nowhere to talk about my adoption. We talked more about the massive argument between my dad and her dad over the whole situation. Her dad did not want me, but wanted my dad to pay for what had happened and to ultimately take me as his responsibility.

I guess I was worth it. Apparently, as I had previously learned, he allowed me to go and live with my biological father after receiving a large sum of money. My parents were by no means rich, but they did own property. As I understood it, this decision set them back basically to ground zero.

For my parents, even owning a home or apartment was a feat, seeing that neither had graduated high school. They were also older and came from a culture where you went to work as early as 9th grade. Although he did not have a lot of formal education, my father was still very smart. He picked up things pretty quickly and had a great business sense, so he always provided for our family.

Our conversation then went on to cover the astonishment of where we were, two sisters talking and giggling like school girls. She started to share about her relationship with Larry and I just listened intently. I felt honored to be trusted enough to be a part of conversations about her personal life.

After, I told her about how I met my husband and our dating for 7 years, before being married at 21. I went on to tell her about being pregnant in high school and how I persevered through college. She told me more about her disconnect with her father and was not surprised about the whole money situation. With another nice conversation behind us, we went back downstairs and then outside.

Alonzo's aunt stated, "You two really look like you could be sisters."

We just looked at each other like two 13-year-olds who had this big inside joke.

Sharon replied, "Really? We look like sisters?" Everyone loved her British accent.

The weekend was going by too fast, and the interesting piece in all of this was how my mom treated her like family as well, as if she was a long-lost relative. I actually noticed the joy in her face when we were together. It was as if she was happy that I was no longer missing out on that part of my life any longer. I finally had the sisters that she could not provide.

My mom would tell Karen, "Come and get some treats from grandma."

She even asked Sharon how her mom was doing and told her to tell her she said hello.

The rest of the weekend flew by, but the time spent was full of warm memories. We took a few photos in the front of our house. Soon, my husband and I had to take Sharon; Larry; her friend, Janet; and Karen back to the airport.

At the airport, we hugged each other in a true sisterly embrace as she said, "Karen, kiss Aunty Lorna goodbye."

It was memories like this that I knew I would cherish forever. As we all grew closer together through communications back and forth, in 2000, I decided to go back to graduate school. I wanted to further my education in the social work and counseling field. My discovery really heightened my exploration of learning more about human development, grief and loss, family history, genograms, and more. It really helped me to look at my adoption through a more comprehensive lens as well.

One class in particular really stuck with me. I had a professor, Winston Johnson, who mentioned how oftentimes there is a family secret. These secrets mean different things, but there is usually one, about abuse, incest, alcoholism, or adoption. He went on to explain how those secrets can become a burden. Therefore, he encouraged us to try to think about what our secrets might be.

As I listened to this professor lecture, I felt like he knew what had happened. Although he was attempting to personalize the issue so that we could understand it better, the drive of his point was to help us work with other families who have these secrets and how this might influence the work we do with them. However, as numerous social workers feel, many in this field, which I was furthering my education in, are wounded healers themselves.

I also always enjoyed science and psychology. The whole nature versus nurture debate continued to fascinate me. Topics such as this in school and my continued journey caused me to constantly look for and try to pinpoint the source of many of my traits and characteristics. Overall, graduate school at Springfield College really helped me to clarify and enhance my interests.

Another great thing about my graduate school experience was that I met two wonderful women, who quickly became my close friends. We connected on a spiritual level, sharing many similarities. Carmen, amazingly enough, was a survivor of years of domestic violence. She was a beautiful, intelligent woman in her late 40s, who seemed to have everything perfectly under control despite her difficult past. Her drive to live, no matter the odds, really inspired me.

My other friend, Gloria, had a similar cultural background as me and some interesting family of origin issues of her own, as I would learn. She came over one day toward the end of my graduate school pursuit. Not too long into her visit, having established such a level of comfort in our friendship already, she began sharing with me how, although she had sisters and brothers, she never quite felt like she belonged. She also told me how her mother callously revealed that her father was not the same father that all of her other siblings had.

She said, "Maybe that is why I feel like I have been treated like an outcast."

Needless to say, it was a very personal and private discussion, and she talked about the Lord placing her in this family and how she and I now seemed to share a sisterly relationship closer than some of her own "blood." The whole time she was talking, I felt a connection to my situation.

Gloria had lived with secrets and family issues for so many years. I felt that I could trust her with my secret in return, especially after she had just opened up and shared with me so much. I did not know how I would feel after sharing it, but I felt the Lord push me forward. This was very new territory for me to explore, but my mind and body did not try to hold me back.

I told her, "I have something I want to share with you, something confidential that I have not been able to share with anyone outside of my husband. However, I feel like the Lord opened the door for me to share today as well."

I then quietly started to tell her the whole story. She just sat in amazement, with tears welled up in her eyes, for at least two hours. It felt like such a relief to share my secret with this sisterly figure who also understood the dynamics of family secrets.

If she were to attend future family functions of mine, I knew that I could trust her in keeping the secret too. I was surprised to feel more freedom than guilt in sharing this secret with another person, as if my entire being let out a sigh of relief. Doing so only brought us closer together as the months continued.

Less than a year after our discussion, I gave my mother

a surprise 70th birthday party. I invited family and friends far and wide, as I really wanted to honor her 70 years on this Earth. When my uncle brought my mom home and we all shouted, "Surprise!" she was so happy that she began to cry.

One of the lingering discrepancies in my quest for answers was still in terms of who really knew the truth of my adoption. There was an older family member there, Aunt June, on my mom's side, who was about 87 years old. Did she know? I really thought she had to.

Aunt June turned emotional after I said, "I just want to help my mother celebrate 70 years. She deserves it."

Apparently once I left her, in response, she turned to Gloria at the party and commented, very unconscientiously, "You know that really is not her daughter."

Gloria, who later described her reaction as her whole body going into shock, responded, "I'm sorry, I didn't hear what you said," and she replied, "Oh nothing, she is a very good daughter."

She later told me that she almost fell off of her chair because she knew I really did not know who was aware of me being adopted. I almost felt like a detective, who was happy and shocked to see a clue slip out so unexpectedly. To think I had wanted to know who knew, but I was unable to just come out and ask anyone. Aunt June's extreme level of joy for what I was doing for my mom on that day gave me a sense that she felt like she was happy how, although not by birth, my mom still had a child that was there for her.

As Aunt June also proved, it was important to know that when you share your secrets, you cannot completely keep them from accidentally spreading. Despite the relief I felt from sharing, I knew my promise and the pros and cons of breaking it. Whenever I became discouraged, I returned to all of the good that came out of my discovery, like my bond with my sisters.

My sister Linda and I continued our written correspondences consistently over the years. She really was a wonderful writer. Her letters were so deep and poetic. She was really a go-getter, traveling to Africa, Egypt, and many other places around the world. I thought she truly lived her life as a real renaissance woman, who knew about so much, not just formal knowledge. She lived her education through museums, trips, reading, but most of all, through living her life.

However, one of the things she had said over the years since I visited, when the topic of her visiting ever came up, was that she did not want to visit under false pretenses. She said that lies had put our relationship behind so many years to begin with, and she did not want to be a part of perpetuating even more of them to whoever I might introduce her to while she was here. I understood, but as I would write to her in response, I did not like to live in a lie either, but I had to respect the reality of the situation.

I had a mother who was actually living with me now, who wanted to maintain that she was my mother. She felt that if I let my children and everyone else know, it would be too much for her to handle.

She would often say, "You can tell everyone when I'm gone."

For that, and for her health alone, she deserved my respect.

Linda also said that she had other concerns. She felt guilty, like she carried the sins of her mother Margaret around with her. She felt it would be hard to be here, worrying how it would make my mother uncomfortable. In response, I told her that when Sharon came, it was actually very comfortable. We chatted and emailed back and forth while she remained unconvinced.

Desperate, I sent one final email attempt to bring her here to visit, stating how if she ever could come, it would be wonderful if she could attend my graduation from graduate school. Although I did not want her to feel pressured, I let her know it would mean a lot to me. She finally seemed receptive and accepted my offer of having a chance to be with her sister on her special day. Thank God she ended up deciding to come! I then focused on graduation, excited and blessed that I had done so well, to be graduating at the top of my class.

A few days before graduation, she arrived. Alonzo and I picked her up at the airport. Amazingly, she had been to the United States once before, and her friend who she happened to know only lived 1.2 miles away from my home. Out of the whole United States, she knew and visited someone who lived just over a mile away! She had been around the corner, so to speak, when I did not even know she existed.

After meeting her friend and his wife, they actually offered to serve as a great connection by bringing gifts over to Margaret and my sisters when they went to visit their family in England. He had no idea that we were sisters, and we just left it that way. They actually mentioned that they wanted to move back to England.

When Linda came into our house, I made sure I introduced her to my mom. However, when she first walked into my home, she stopped dead in her tracks. As it turned out, I had the exact artwork that she had on the wall in her living room, on my wall in my living room. My mom smiled and gave her a big hug. She also met Alicia and Ashley.

I mentioned how this was a special piece of art we had.

She joked and said, "Is yours signed personally by the artist?"

I laughed and said, "Okay, maybe yours is a tad different."

We laughed at yet another "ordaincident."

I was reminded again just how funny she was, which did not translate as well in written communications. She was very clever with her jokes, humor, and frankness. She also helped to do anything that needed to be done; she did not want to be seen as a guest. Each day, she was the first one up, going for walks and being busy as a bee in the house. She behaved like a loving sister would have. I could not have been more thankful for the warm conversations we shared.

On the day of graduation, we all got up ready to get

dressed. My family and I had picked out our color scheme for our clothes based on the pink and black dress and shoes I had. This had been decided a few weeks prior, as we wanted to feel united and coordinated on this special day.

We showered and dressed. When Linda came into my room to help, I could not believe my eyes! She had come in wearing a pink and black top and a black skirt. It was to the point where I came to accept these astounding moments without much question now.

When we finally got to the venue, I memorably introduced her as my younger sister to my other school colleagues who did not know my family. I told everyone she traveled all of the way from England. People were so welcoming, and Gloria could not wait to meet her.

The only people who probably had questions were my mother's family, who were aware of most of our family members. When put on the spot by them that day, I told them that she was from my father's side, because I did not have as many relatives on his side living close by. However, I could still sense a general "who is that again" inquiry.

It felt great to graduate, to have come such a long way in my life and to celebrate such an achievement with my classmates, friends, and family. After the celebrating was over, the next day we spent time with Gloria and a friend of hers who had also came up for her graduation. The four of us went to the Mashantucket Pequot Museum and Research Center together, and we just talked about what we saw, laughed, ate at a restaurant, and enjoyed being together.

Gloria commented, "You can tell you are sisters."

I enjoyed the level of openness we could have while Linda was visiting, acting on the truth of our existence, as the cloud that had been above my life, my secret, continued to dissipate. I liked the feeling of being free. In the end, we appreciated getting to know each other more as sisters, for who we really were. When

Linda left, she was glad that she had come and we had every intention of continuing to build upon our relationship for as long as possible.

-CHAPTER 12-
MEMORABLE GIFTS

My daughter Alicia was still in college when her fiancé Lamont, who was in the military, proposed to her. She was at the end of her Junior Year at Rutgers. He had went to Alonzo and respectfully asked for his blessing, and he happily gave it to him. From that point on, we were starting to plan; even though she was still young, we knew she was ready.

Not before long, we were very deep into wedding planning, discussing guests and other details. Once I came to terms that she would be living in England, it was clear to me that I would need to tell her the truth. However, I wanted to wait until right after her wedding.

I told Margaret, Sharon, and Linda about the upcoming nuptials. I really hoped that Margaret could attend, but I knew there was a slim chance since she had told me before she had no interest in flying. Ever since 9/11, she was still a bit nervous.

Although it seemed out of character, with her so fearless when it came to many other things, I respected her decision. The other theory was that she had not revealed my birth to her then fiancé and to make a trip to the United States for a wedding for someone not immediately related may be difficult to explain. This was just another possible scenario my sisters and I surmised. Either way, I would not push her, but made sure she was asked and felt welcomed.

I had also told both my sisters that I would share the news with my oldest daughter after the wedding. They were a little surprised and wondered how I would approach it and how she might, in turn, receive it. I wrote back that I was not sure, God only knows, but I did know I had to tell her before she left.

I thought it would simply be amazing to have all of us together at such a major life event. I also knew that the timing and costs had to be justifiable for everyone. The flights to the United States were not cheap and arrangements also had to be made at our places of work. I thought about the wedding and the discussion that would follow many times over before either occurred.

A month before the wedding, Sharon told me that she and Karen would be attending! They would stay for two weeks. It was going to be great to have them here. Karen was already almost four and also very intelligent. She spoke like a six or seven-year-old and her word recognition was amazing. As she would be here during her birthday, I was already planning for a small party. It would be a fun, small gathering with cake for our immediate family.

Linda, unfortunately, was dealing with some restructuring at her job. She too worked in the "helping others" field and had a lot of work to do in dealing with a recent tsunami and other issues. She was worried that her employer might face cutbacks or layoffs due to resulting changes.

Sadly, Linda let me know she could not make it. Although I was a little disappointed, I understood. Plus, she had just come the year before for my graduation. It would be Sharon's turn, her second visit to see me in the United States.

A few days before the wedding, Sharon and Karen arrived. After I got out of the heavy traffic I was stuck in, I picked them up. There were still a lot of "to dos" in preparation for Alicia's big day. Despite being anxious, I was still so happy to see them both.

Karen exclaimed "Hi Aunty Lorna, I am going to the wedding!"

I told her, "Yes you are! I know you already have a dress, but Aunty Lorna bought a pretty dress for you too, so you have two dresses to choose from for it."

During the time they were here, we went to the dress rehearsal together, got our dresses together, and behaved like two sisters. I was an aunt, a sister, and a mother who wanted to have everything go perfectly. This trip, there were no questions; we were just being family.

They met my son-in-law, his family, and my in-laws. Once again, I could say they were on my father's side. However, the one close uncle I had on my father's side was also invited to the wedding and was planning to attend. It would be interesting to see how that went.

His planned presence there reminded me of an incident I had when he was invited to my oldest daughter's high school graduation in 2001. After graduation, we had a small party at our home.

After the celebration, Uncle Vernon pulled me aside and said, "Before I leave, I want to talk with you privately."

I replied, "We can talk as we walk outside."

He whispered, "I have something I need to tell you."

He did not get any further when it hit me that he knew, and he was about to tell me.

I interrupted him in anticipation, replying, "I know what you are going to say, but tell me anyway."

He continued, "Well, your father is your father, but your mother is not."

I responded, "I know."

Shocked, he replied, "You do? How?" at which point I told him the abbreviated version of my discovery, but explained how only my husband knew, so mum's the word.

Preparations flew by and before I knew it the guests were arriving, including Uncle Vernon with his wife and my two cousins, Kim and Michael. The wedding was unquestionably beautiful.

During the following reception, Uncle Vernon saw Sharon sitting at the head table with me. Each step he took toward us, he kept looking at her in awe.

He finally came over and I said, again in anticipation, "Yes, this is my sister."

He was so fascinated, in a genuine enthrallment.

I thought to myself, "Thank God someone would have the knowledge and courage to share the truth with me had I not found out in the mail on that fateful day."

I could rest assured knowing that I would have found out one way or the other eventually. Finding out through him though made me question how things would have been different. However, in the end, everything was happening as it was meant to be. Although I was nervous, I knew my next step would be sharing my secret, the truth, with Alicia.

After I did, I was fortunate that Alicia had handled it so well. My accidental discovery of my adoption continued to bring with it both tangible and intangible gifts and memories, with surprisingly few negative experiences outside of having to live a life of secrecy with many. One of the best physical gifts I had ever received was from Linda, who had become such a talented family historian. One day, I went to the mailbox and there was a package. I opened it to find a detailed scrapbook, with all of these lovingly placed photos and handwritten notes in it.

Most striking was the cover, a vintage photo of the back of three women sitting on the beach with sun hats. Inside she wrote, three from one. This beautiful expression of love and understanding through the sharing of lost history meant so much to me. The contents also provided me with a visual family tree of our other immediate relatives.

As I poured over the pages, slowly taking in each photo and reading each letter, I found myself laughing and crying and laughing again. There were pictures of uncles, cousins, grandparents, her, Margaret, Sharon, and nieces. There were pictures of

Margaret in her 20s, 30s, 40s, 50s, and from her 60th birthday.

She detailed Margaret's personality in wonderful, colorful stories. As I read them, I discovered so many additional, amazing similarities that I shared with her. She indicated how I inherited that pre-planning and taking-care-of-business gene, as she called it. What a way to bring me up to speed, a gift that I knew would be handed down for a lifetime; she had a very wise countenance.

Another gift given by Linda was less tangible, but just as significant as a family history on paper. In August 2007, my mother decided she had not been to England in over 20 years. Although her health was not the best, knee replacements and the onset of dementia, her doctor approved her to travel. We had secured a passport for her and got her packed up to go and visit her brother, as well as friends she had long left behind. I had informed Margaret that my mom would be over there and told her my mom hoped they could connect. They had spoken on the phone a couple of times over the years, but this would be their first encounter in over 40 years.

We took my mother to the airport and sent her on her way with her brother, to reconnect with her English roots. She was staying with him and her sister-in-law for a week. Shortly after her arrival, she called Margaret to invite her to my aunt and uncle's house. Margaret, Linda, Vanessa, and the children then proceeded to take several trains, but finally made it to the house.

Linda recounted how they had a nice exchange, although I wondered if my aunt knew who she was, as they said she did not respond that welcoming to their visit. My mom was always a very hospitable hostess and seeing this bothered her, but she and Margaret at least had a chance to connect like two old friends catching up. My mother called me after their visit the next day and told me about the exchange. I was so happy they were able to meet.

My mother also shared that her leg was hurting her, and I suggested she go and have it checked out at the hospital. When she went there, she had to be hospitalized for what turned out to be a blood clot. This was due to the long plane ride.

She contacted me to deal with the hospital, as I had managed her healthcare back home. I worked with the doctor to ensure she was receiving proper treatment and sent over all of her information. She stayed there for a few weeks as we communicated with her brother, the hospital, and tried to figure out the best course of action.

She was getting irritable, partially due to not being home and being sick, but the early onset of dementia was creating an added irritability in her personality. I had to explain this to her caregivers to put it in perspective. Finally, the hospital released her and authorized her ability to fly home.

Alonzo and I were trying to figure out who could come back with her, because her brother could not bring her. We did not have the time from work available at that point, as we had just returned off vacation. In case we had to travel internationally, I had actually gone and renewed my passport, a process that was a lot less involved this time around. I was also now a U.S. citizen and there would be no secrets to be revealed.

One day, I was sharing with Linda the details of this difficult situation. Although I was nervous to ask, as this was a big deal to ask someone to leave their home to accompany someone they really did not know that well and fly almost 3,500 miles to the United States, I barely got the question out and she stated that as long as she could work out the details of her holiday, she would do it.

I was so happy and overjoyed that she was offering to help my mother get back safely to our home. I told her that I would make all of the arrangements and pay for her fare, as not to be too much of an unexpected burden on her. We booked the plane tickets, and I sent over the information.

Linda was so patient and kind with my mother and took such good care of her as they traveled. "Ms. Alice," as she would call her, had every need met, and my mother and I got to see just how patient and caring Linda truly was.

Once she arrived at the airport, my mother just kept saying, "She is so sweet and loving. Your sister is so nice, such a nice girl."

She was so enamored with her, and I was amazed at how life continued to have an ever-winding road of surprises: My mother being cared for and supported by the daughter of someone she may have once despised; Margaret and my mother speaking on the phone and coming to a place where they now said love you to each other; My mother and Linda developing a mutual admiration for one another; Sharon and Karen calling my mom Grandma Alice; and more. All I can say is that this journey of discoveries continued to be one that felt like a "Lifetime" movie, if I ever saw one. My life was now rich with miracles, faith, and love. I was truly blessed.

-CHAPTER 13-
GOING HOME - HOME GOING

Sadly, my dear mother, who I was raised by, who had lived with my husband and me since 1998, died as I was contemplating how to bring this book to a close. It was as if her passing signaled it was time for me to hurry up and reach my conclusion. She had known that I had shared our secret with some immediate family, and I planned to one day write this very book.

She and I were both put through a lot, especially from 1997 to 2013. I had come to understand that all of the choices made prior to my awareness of my unknown heritage were outside of my control. It made me really take to the Bible scripture Psalm 139:13-14: "For you created my inmost being; you knit me together in my mother's womb. I praise you because I am fearfully and wonderfully made; your works are wonderful, I know that full well."

A main driving force in putting this story to paper had been the realization that I would one day have to share my secret with my youngest daughter and wanted to put my thoughts together cohesively for when I felt she was ready. The moment my mother took her last breath, I realized I would need to take my first without her and will myself to tell this truth to my youngest child and to whoever else I felt was ready for it. However, as there was so much grief and emotion after the death of my mother, and with my daughter in college, I did not want her distracted from her studies.

My mother had also died two days before my birthday. Prior to this, I had spoken to Margaret to exchange birthday greetings. She called me again the following day, which was unusual, as we did not talk so frequently, just to ask if everything was okay. I questioned if someone had informed her of the news, and she replied along the lines of, informed her of what? I then told her how my mother had passed away the day before.

She was so saddened as she responded, "My Lord, I felt that something was wrong and that is why I called you."

I could not believe that she had sensed something and felt the need to call me. Meanwhile, with the entire funeral planning and heartache, the need to get away and breathe became stronger than ever. During one call, she coincidentally invited us to visit her seasonal home in Jamaica, and although she had invited us previously, and we had not gone, this time it was impossible to say no.

I also thought this would be a good time to have the girls greet and meet their other grandmother, both aware and without confliction this time. We waited until Spring Break, where there would be a free moment for all of us. Unfortunately, due to the terrible winter storms, high school vacation was cancelled, and therefore, Alonzo being a teacher could not attend.

In preparation, I called Ashley and told her that I really wanted to talk to her when she came home. I think she sensed it was important, but I believe she felt it would probably be about the rules and expectations after she graduated from college. Surely, she had no idea of the topic to come. While on the phone, she did not ask many questions, which was a relief.

Leading up to the day she would come home, I found myself reliving all of the emotions I experienced in telling Alicia years before. My heart raced once again, and I felt nervous about the risk for this upcoming revelation to somehow cause unnecessary hurt or pain. Alonzo and I paced and prayed for days that she would take the news as well as her sister did.

When she finally came home, we told her to come and sit down.

She responded, "I knew you wanted to talk to me, but I didn't think it was a serious matter. Is it bad news; is someone ill?"

We said the news can be seen as good or bad, but no one was ill.

Soon, as the words began to slip out of my mouth once more, "Your grandmother that you have always known is your adoptive grandmother," I saw the look of confusion and shock take control of her face.

She just sat in silence for a moment as she tried to make sense of the information we were just now sharing with her. Her emotions felt familiar, as I had experienced them before as well.

She questioned, "How could that be?"

I explained all of the details as a single tear fell down her face; she, in her usual caring way, asked me, "How do you feel about this?"

I told her, "I am at peace with the information."

Ashley responded thoughtfully and appeared pensive during our conversation. She was very close to my mother and this news was being shared only two months after her death. My very sensitive and intuitive child handled the release of the secret in a very secure manner.

She then commented in a manner of amazement, "This is crazy, your life is like a 'Lifetime' movie."

My husband and I just looked at each other in agreement. I told her the good thing is she would have an opportunity to meet Margaret in just a couple of days, as her granddaughter now. This unknown family member would have a face, voice, and now become known as who she really was. I had such a sense of relief when the conversation concluded and the secret had now been revealed to all of those closest to me. She had been the last person who I had the most concern about telling, as it directly impacted her life, her existence, and our shared history.

I prayed that our subsequent trip would be a lot less stressful than our first visit to England. This would be just my second face-to-face meeting with Margaret. More excited than anything, my family packed our bags and boarded the plane for Montego Bay, Jamaica.

As we experienced a slight delay, we hoped that she would not be too inconvenienced. We were excited to be going away, as I had not been to Jamaica in over 20 years. I had been so busy with work, school, and family that going away internationally was up until now unfathomable.

When we landed at the airport, we went to pick up our luggage. We called to indicate that we had arrived at the airport; her voice on the other line sounded elated. The humid hot air, the trees, and the sea of Jamaican accents pleasantly let us know we were far from home.

We went outside and started looking for the car she described. Before we knew it, I saw her walking to us!

She said from a distance, "Hello my darlings."

I was busy watching the reaction of the girls, because although my oldest had met her in England, we had never all been together before now. They watched as she easily strolled up to the sidewalk to greet us. She had on leggings, sandals, and a colorful top as she moved as quickly as we did. After hugs, which my body had once again became full of glowing energy for, we all got into the car.

In the car, we met a friend of hers who would be driving us to her home inside a gated community near the town of Ocho Rios. Although we were very tired, we took time to take in all of the tropical scenery. It was a beautiful, two-hour trip from the airport to the house. The time flew by with beautiful visuals. We passed areas that were very traditional "country," and we also passed some of the new gated communities that were also emerging in the area.

We were very excited. When we passed the row of majestic palm trees, I could not help but notice how they so lovingly lined the entrance to the nicely landscaped gated community. Our arrival at her home was an opportunity to take family photos, even though our tiredness was increasingly setting in.

The girls took photos with Margaret, and we took some together, as again we did not know if we would ever have this moment again. She hugged us so tight and stated how happy she was to have us all together. After all of this time, everyone was finally together and in a sunny, warm, and relaxing environment. I wished Sharon and Linda were also there with us, but I knew it would be challenging to have all of us clear our schedules and priorities at the same time.

When I went to sit down in the living room, I noticed some 8x10 and 5x7 photos of my sisters and me. I had a photo by myself and my sisters had individual ones and one they both had taken together as teens. There was also a family photo that my husband and I had taken with the kids, on display on the living room table.

My first thought was that I did not have to be hidden in this environment. I was a known part of the equation. It made me wonder if her friends who she shared five months a year with in Jamaica wondered why there were no photos of her three daughters together. I thought she must feel good about being able to freely talk about her daughters and her grandchildren now.

This visit provided another level of freedom to be who we really were. After relaxing at the pool, she invited us to visit a neighbor. Margaret was soon busy introducing us. She quickly shared what she had told her friend about us living in the United States, possibly as not to have conflicting stories with any questions her friend may have.

She commented, "I want you to meet my daughter and my granddaughters."

I could see the look of joy on her face, being able to share what was becoming increasingly less of a secret. My body finally felt a true release too in hearing Margaret refer to me as a daughter in public. We were there as who we really were.

It was even more thrilling to hear her neighbor Felicia, say, "Oh, nice to meet you; I've heard so much about you!"

In my mind, I thought, "I hope she doesn't ask too many questions."

However, those became fleeting thoughts, as I was pleased to feel so relaxed and at ease. I watched as my children cautiously embraced this title of "my granddaughters" with someone other than the grandmother they had always known.

During the remainder of our time together, we would consciously and subconsciously absorb the essence of one another. We were busy observing and catching up on the nuances that most people in familial relationships often take for granted. It was a time of looking at patterns of behavior and seeing if and how they connect back to who we are.

We were awed by Margaret's energy in especially how she got up early in the morning to plant and clean up her garden, after doing a 5:30 am workout at the complex's outdoor gym; her immense level of liveliness and physical ability for a woman in her late 60s; her being a social butterfly; and her having friendships throughout the entire neighborhood. The more we were together, the more we all saw ourselves in one another. The location and what was happening in it could not have been more beautiful.

It was so funny to experience her feistiness and wit amidst all of her friends who were there as retirees, many from other countries who had come back home, to Jamaica, to live. They were all a spirited and fun-loving group in the midst of being very traditional and proper.

Of the many activities during our visit, one that was very memorable to me was our trip to Mystic Mountain. We went on a bobsled ride where we had to ride the skyline to get to the top of the mountain. My girls were on one seat together and Margaret and I went on another. The ride was a slow and scary one, as it was a misty day and we were hundreds of feet up in the air. There would also be no exiting out of any conversations en route.

As we rode up the mountain, she began to share that she was so happy that we were able to come and have this time together. In these moments, I decided to ask a few questions and get some final clarity. I did not know if it was brought on by being up near the heavens, the picturesque view, or the feeling of being so safe with one another that moved me to ask them.

She honestly shared how difficult her life had been ever since the conception had occurred. She cried as she told me that her husband was an abusive, controlling, and mean person.

She stated, "He forced me to give you to your dad. He would have hurt us all if I didn't make that choice. He hurt us all anyway."

What she said reminded me of her words the day before, how "it's only by God's grace why I am alive and have not gone mad with the things I went through at that time," which had been brought on by the video tribute from my mom's funeral that I had shown her.

The tribute had old photos in it with my mom and dad that she had not seen in so long or had never seen before. Margaret had been in a daze as she watched the video and teared up to it, I initially thinking it was only due to my mom's death. On the ride, she clarified it was both her passing and seeing the photos that brought her back to such a painful time in her life.

She said, "I was in a bad place when all that happened, and I am glad we are where we are supposed to be now. Thank the Lord".

I had long since moved past anger, blame, and judgment on the matter. I actually felt her pain when she shared these words and the accompanying emotions they carried. Her strength to overcome a mentally and sometimes physically-abusive relationship by deciding to divorce in an era where women stayed with their husbands regardless of circumstance was very impressive.

Her resilience and independent spirit was refreshing, and I was quite sure there were aspects that I could never connect with; however, we met each other this second time as adults and did not have to deal with adolescent parent/child friction. We did not have to interact on a day-to-day basis where those idiosyncrasies ever got in the way. Although she could be opinionated and speak her mind, I was not offended by her style. I recognized that whenever we got together, it would most likely be a positive experience, as we both wanted things to work out between us, and we undeniably had a lot of similarities.

Both of my girls were also fortunate to have spent some time alone with her and came to know her much better during that too-short, five-day visit. They were happy for the experience and the vacation away from the day-to-day.

We were all only three months into our grief process, yet we had an opportunity to be blessed with a newness of life and truthful relationships. The trip helped me to better understand the complexity of the circle of life and how we lost someone special, yet we gained another special person in our lives. I loved Margaret like a mother, and she loved me like a daughter. I could not have asked for a better outcome.

-CHAPTER 14-
PARTING THOUGHTS

I watched Darryl McDaniels's Emmy-winning VH1 documentary "D.M.C.: My Adoption Journey." Ironically, I interviewed Darryl while he was touring as a member in Run–D.M.C.. As it turned out, we had a shared history without even knowing it at the time.

When I saw the previews, the story of this Hip Hop legend, it immediately peaked my interest as it sounded so familiar. As I watched this hour-long glimpse, I connected deeply with the emotions he experienced in so many ways. The shock after finding out the issues associated with searching for his mother, the waiting, and the disappointments were all similar feelings I had experienced as well. The courage he displayed by sharing his personal story truly inspired me.

Before my daughters knew, I also thought back to our entire family watching the episode "Secrets and Lies," of the show "Moesha," starring Brandy Norwood. In it, it was revealed Moesha's cousin Dorian was actually her father Frank's son. Frank had sent him to live with his sister, who had raised him as her own.

I remember bracing myself for my children's thoughts, comments, and reactions about the situation that had transpired onscreen. They in turn expressed how upset they would be and how these families were now all mixed up. Needless to say, popular culture's view on adoption is still one that is very emotional and hard to comprehend or sometimes accept.

As the draft of this memoir sat on the shelf in my bedroom closet since it was initially written in 2005, while I was recovering in my house from a surgery, things have only continued to change. Since the beginning of the process, where a secret became revealed, I witnessed the relationship with my birth mother and sisters evolve into something where I was not searching for anything anymore. Today, I am comfortable with just being.

There is no need to talk to my siblings or Margaret as often as possible now; as long as I know that they are there, who they are, I am at peace. You might think there would have been many trips since and nonstop conversations, but there has instead been a sense of security that allows me to be at peace with just the fact of having found my needle in a haystack and that needle, in turn, receiving me so openly. When we do communicate, our messages, phone calls, and visits in-between continue to provide for an even greater connection.

As everyone goes through their connection points with a newly found family, I recognize that each person will deal with those relationships differently, and what works for one, may not work for others. For example, I enjoyed my new relationships as they began to settle, be discovered, and grow. On one occasion, a cousin who lived only a couple of hours from me called and eagerly wanted to visit as soon as she learned about me. It made me realize how I had initially only been focused on my immediate family members in England and didn't even think to connect with others, partly fueled by my concern as to how I would introduce them to my local community, as well as not knowing who knew what.

Although I had indicated it was a difficult time for me, due to it being right on the heels of my mother-in-law's death, I decided to meet with her. It was a time filled with a lot of emotion, and I did not know how to feel an instant connection. This was not due to a lack of caring or desire, but my pause made me realize how everyone is in a different position as he or she begins to meet family. During our visit, I still felt unsure, as I, at the time, subconsciously did not want her to reveal to others how we were related.

These different speeds people move at during the post-discovery timeframe is like having a dance partner, where you are both doing the same dance, but moving in different directions and at different speeds. In all honesty, my oldest daughter Alicia, who had spent over 20 years with my mother as her grandma, is still not as eager to move forward with a relationship with her biological grandmother.

She was fortunate enough to visit and spend a little time with her grandmother and aunts during her stay in England. She actually attended Margaret's 60th birthday party and commented on her energetic and social spirit. She also described it as being a voyeur, looking into someone else's life, while she watched the celebration. It was also a little easier then, as my mother was still alive.

Alicia's slow pace for connection has nothing to do with Margaret, but more to do with how she feels about entering into this new relationship, which gives her complex and mixed emotions, some of the same ones I had felt with other family members. I actually had to learn not to prompt her to contact Margaret, as she was an adult and would connect in her own time.

I have just wanted to make sure my children know such an opportunity for connection will not last forever, as Margaret is aging and the hands of time will not return. During post-discovery, regardless of the decision anyone makes, the key is to be comfortable with your decision to move fast, slow, or not at all. Facebook has also helped me meet extended family members on my timeframe; some even unwittingly having me share too much, as I thought they already knew. I am just now ready to actively seek a relationship with additional family members who live in the Boston area. Change takes time.

I find myself oftentimes returning to those important moments that have transpired since I found out the truth, such as the opportunity to have my adoptive mother meet Margaret, mummy, when she visited England. It was a healing meeting that was filled with joy, hope, and catharsis. I had the delight of hearing the relief in both of their voices that there was no animosity toward each other, just a shared child who had the benefit of now having two wonderful mothers.

I also learned firsthand about compassion and how to love a child who is not born to you, as my family took on the care of an 17-year-old young woman, with a son. Her mother and all other family members lived in another country, and she had an incredibly difficult and abusive childhood. I never thought I would open my home and my life to another, but this was meant to be.

I realized I mother young women on a regular basis as an Executive Director of a group home for pregnant and parenting young women, but becoming a mother of another person provided another perspective on motherly love. She is my third daughter, Donisha and I am her mother. My husband, now her father, and we are proudly the grandparents of our little amazing grandson Xavier.

Furthermore, in 2010, I took a year-long, post-Masters class, on foster and adoption studies, where I also realized my job as Executive Director of St. Agnes Home was also connected way beyond why I thought I was there. At first, I mainly thought that this connection was due to me having a child as a teen, being a leader and role model who could understand what these young women were experiencing. Regarding its history, the early foundation of St. Agnes Home was as an orphanage where many young women had babies and placed them up for adoption. As it turned out, my experience with adoption and searching prepared me to be especially empathetic to the many that come by the home, searching for their own birth-parents.

I did not have my true ah-ha moment until 2012, when a couple came in after her husband found out he was adopted. This revelation only came about after his parents died and they found some adoption paperwork. This, in actuality, is a common occurrence, the hidden secrecy of adoption.

We sat down and met. He shared such powerful and meaningful information with me as he thanked us for having a home like St. Agnes Home where he had the chance to be born and then adopted into a loving family. He broke down into tears, for the first time in his marriage, as he wife noted.

In that moment, I was one with his pain, understanding his sense of the surreal. I instinctually put my hand over his and told him how these feelings were normal. He apologized unknowing why he was crying, but I more than understood and was able to provide some comfort as they visited the place where he had just learned his journey began.

It became clear that day why I was there. I was there to provide hope for the young moms who want to be able to parent and also be a source of strength, courage, and understanding for those who were adopted from St. Agnes Home, as well as those who placed a child and were trying to locate him/her. My gift was an added connection to those who find out accidently. At times, I have felt guilty not being able to reveal our shared situations, so that when I state I know it must be difficult going through this process, I can actually provide a personal experience. I am happy I can share now.

As I think about how destiny and fate worked out, I cannot help but return once more to "The Purpose Driven Life: What on Earth am I Here For?," by Dr. Rick Warren. His message remains so powerful, as it reinforces that my birth and adoption, although complex, was ordained. My life was turning out as it was supposed to. Although it can be difficult for someone in such a situation to come to terms with it, it is important for one to believe and accept that fact.

This notion of predestiny can even be extended to Alicia, who got married to a military man, at the time stationed overseas in England. Previously, he had also been in the United States and to Japan. His location, combined with the timing of the revelation, still feels so right.

My story will now be shared with the largest audience ever, and although it will provide answers for many, it will provide more questions for others. In 2005, I remember having a reccurring vision of being on the Oprah Winfrey show and telling her my story, but I always had a veil over my face, as I could not let anyone know who I was.

This story was being told in anonymity, and Oprah then tells me, "You can't tell your story unless you are able to tell it freely."

That is why I was in tears when I saw the show where her sister Pat shared her story; I kept saying, "Even Oprah experienced what I have dealt with."

While I may have changed some names, I want to reiterate that everything I have shared is true and the cloud has now been lifted. I have tried to provide a sense of who people are without directly identifying those who may not be willing participants, but this is my truth and I myself was placed into this story without consent. There are memories I have not shared, but every story of every interaction is not necessary to understand who I am today and grasp the underlying feelings and messages inside my words.

I have shared knowing that it may be hard for some to understand my need to dispel this cloud of secrecy once and for all. For those of you that know me personally, please know that my not sharing this information with you wasn't done with an intent to deceive, but from a place of respect for my mother's wishes. So many of you have played an important role in my life and your presence has impacted my unbelievable journey, even though you were unaware of your role.

I also believe in being authentic, and this allows me to live up to my whole truth. I am blessed to have had a second chance to build a relationship with my birth mother, Margaret, the one who provided me with her genetics, while I had an opportunity to become the closest to my mother I had ever been toward the end of her life. Through nature and nurture, I am free to be. I honored my mother's wishes and remained silent during her lifetime.

With that said, I hope my story brings to you, the reader, some insight into the journey one might take when forced to live under the cloud of any secret or when found thrown in the midst of any difficult situation. Whether you are an interested reader, an adoptee, an adopter, or living with a secret, truth is always a critical component in making the journey easier. Truth, no matter how hard, gives journeys in life direction. Stories like this date back as far as Exodus. The Bible detailed adoption through Moses, including family secrets, how he was with his mother, who had to give him away in order to save him.

Regarding the unforgettable scrapbook from my sister Linda, a photo of the cover has been included in this very book. It is easy to tell she placed a lot of thought into it, with careful attention to detail. For each person, she tried to find out about their character, employment, personality, and more. The cover of the scrapbook is symbolic and still holds true, those three women with sun hats and bathing suits, sitting on the beach, faced by a mom, representing the three of us still to this day. Each page continues to give me new information about my biological family and how, although I have not been a known part of it for very long, I have definitely become a part of it now.

With my revelation to Ashley, this same scrapbook was shared with her, along with an earlier draft of this book. I actually passed both books onto her as I finally shared my secret. Although every mum will someday fade, it is the memories and stories that can live forever.

I release my secret happily, healthy in mind, body, and spirit. I came out of this process whole, with the gap that had been created when I found out about my adoption since largely filled. Life is a journey. Enjoy it for as long as you can. Just remember how everyone is impacted when life forces one to "Mum's the Word."

-My Letters-

A letter to my Mom...

Dear Mom,

Thank you so much for loving my father enough to accept and take on the responsibility of being the mother for a child born out of a situation that must have caused you pain. Things weren't always easy with an independent and strong-minded child, who probably reminded you of my dad being with someone else. I know that I was a daddy's girl, but I always loved you too.

It must have also been hard to deal with the burden of infertility in an era where a woman was defined by motherhood. Please forgive yourself for any shame you held, as you prayed for a child, and although the method of delivery wasn't what you had planned, your prayers were answered. I realize that you being there during my pregnancy, with me being a young parent, provided you with some experiences as it relates to caring for a newborn.

I know I was initially mad about you not telling me about my adoption, but know that I have moved beyond that anger to a sense of gratefulness. I thank you for raising me and loving me until your passing. I am so happy that you could always depend on me, your only child, as I managed all of your affairs to ensure your care, especially as you became increasingly immobile, due to failing health. I loved seeing your smile whenever you exhibited your pride in me; I so wish you were with me when I met Oprah.

I also want to thank you for your expressions of joy in your granddaughters and their academic pursuits. They loved their GaGa, and you loved them back. Your legacy lives on through all of your life lessons and phrases, such as you teaching me the importance of prayer and the value of please and thank you. My resilience and healing journey since learning of this secret was due to the strength you instilled, through prayers, forgiveness, and gratitude, all things gained from your nurturing.

Thank you, we love you, and we miss you.

A letter to my Daughters...

My Daughters,

I have always wanted the best for you: mind, body, and spirit. Please forgive me for being the keeper of the secret for so long. I held onto it at the request of your grandmother, because in part she never wanted this information to change the feelings you had toward and for her. Although I haven't known this information throughout your entire lives, what I do know is how I feel about it, being your mother, and what I want for you.

I was blessed to have two children conceived in love, and much later in life, a third also achieved by love. I am thankful to see you all grow and achieve a life that is bigger than that of mine and either of your grandmothers, a life freer from the societal, economic, and emotional boundaries that we had to manage. May the memories you have of me, your mother, be that she dared to dream and achieve, while making sure her girls were afforded every opportunity to be who they were meant to be: confident, smart, creative, beautiful, and God-loving young women.

I am thankful that you were there, in your unknowing, to provide me with the motivation to maintain a steady state, as I sought out our roots and replanted my own foundation. Your grandmother lived to see and experience mothering through loving and cherishing you all during her life. Alicia, you were the only one who got to meet your grandfather, as he died at 65, before any secret was told.

At the end of GaGa's life, she was happy to know that there was another layer of love left for us. This book was written to provide us with the freedom to assume our full identities. Let us be grateful and thankful for being resilient and loving women, who grew together beyond secrets and silence into our true selves. We're free!

I will always love you.

-RESOURCES-

If you are an adoptee or a birthparent planning on an adoption search and hopeful to have a family reunion, there is no such thing as too much planning. The time to start preparing for an adoption reunion is actually way before you start your actual adoption search. It is important to understand that the timeframe for a search can range from days to years. Be aware that the legal access to some aspects your information may also impact your search

Once you make the decision and begin an adoption search the process can be quite consuming. To go from wondering about your birth family to actually taking action is an exhilarating and emotional step. Every individual and every situation is different, although we often share similar themes within the adoption spectrum. Just as I spent time reading about adoption reunions, it is important to read and gain insight and knowledge from other people's experiences. Processing the differing perspectives and different outcomes in each situation may prepare you for your potential reunion. Make sure you read adoption stories from the adoptee's point of view and read adoption reunion stories told form the birthmother or birthfather's point of view. It is very important to be aware of positive family reunion stories and also the reunions that didn't work out as desired. Don't hesitate to seek professional guidance to help you through the journey.

Blessings!

www.adoption.com • www.adopting.org
www.davethomasfoundation.org • www.laura-dennis.com
www.americanadoptioncongress.com

*A **Mum's the Word** accompanying workbook for schools of social work, adoption certificate, and human service programs in addition to all professionals working with someone in the adoption constellation is available.

www.mumsthewordbook.com

19087377R00084

Made in the USA
Middletown, DE
03 April 2015